Strategic Sustainable Supply Chain Management

Strategic Sustainable Supply Chain Management

Foundations

Robert P. Sroufe and Steven A. Melnyk

BEP
BUSINESS EXPERT PRESS
Leader in applied, concise business books

Strategic Sustainable Supply Chain Management: Foundations

Copyright © Business Expert Press, LLC, 2025

Cover design by Charlene Kronstedt

Interior design by Exeter Premedia Services Private Ltd., Chennai, India

First published in 2013 by
Business Expert Press, LLC
222 East 46th Street, New York, NY 10017
www.businessexpertpress.com

ISBN-13: 978-1-63742-762-0 (paperback)
ISBN-13: 978-1-63742-763-7 (e-book)

Business Expert Press Environmental and Social Sustainability for
Business Advantage Collection

Third edition: 2025

10 9 8 7 6 5 4 3 2 1

EU SAFETY REPRESENTATIVE
Mare Nostrum Group B.V.
Mauritskade 21D
1091 GC Amsterdam
The Netherlands
gpsr@mare-nostrum.co.uk

Description

This 3rd edition book provides a multiperspective approach to strategic sustainability and value chains to allow understanding from various disciplines and professional backgrounds.

Some of the key features of this first volume include a how-to guide on *foundational information* for strategic sustainable supply chain management (S3CM):

- Short vignettes of important trends along with relevant management issues
- Evidence-based management examples from leading multinational companies, as well as small and medium enterprises spanning supply chains
- Reference to appropriate tools, emerging technology, and practices
- Chapter action items for the reader to take a deeper look at integration opportunities involving sustainability and supply chain management
- An action-learning approach to applying concepts and tools so readers from any functional perspective can implement and manage sustainability projects
- And guidelines on how to move forward with your supply chain sustainability initiative

Contents

The flow of chapter information in this book:

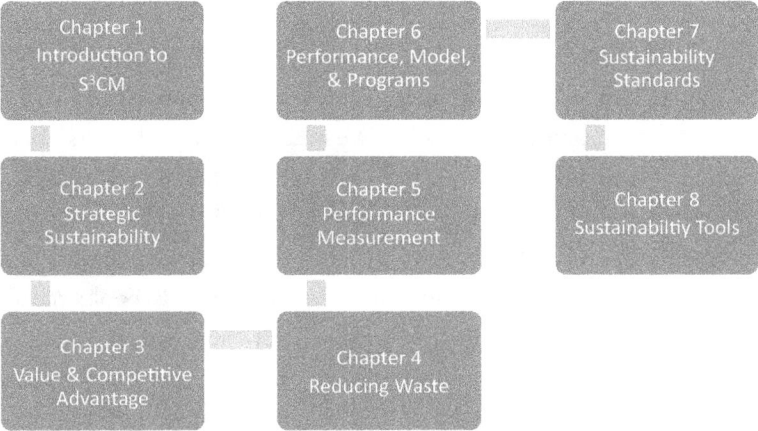

Chapter 1 Introduction to S³CM	**Chapter 6** Performance, Model, & Programs	**Chapter 7** Sustainability Standards
Chapter 2 Strategic Sustainability	**Chapter 5** Performance Measurement	**Chapter 8** Sustainabiltiy Tools
Chapter 3 Value & Competitive Advantage	**Chapter 4** Reducing Waste	

Acknowledgments

We would like to thank the many people and organizations that contributed their support to this book. We need to thank MBA students for pushing out thinking and Graduate Assistants for their research assistance and refinement of the chapters. Next, we would like to thank Chatham University; the Alcoa Foundation for funding a fellowship program and portions of the research within earlier versions of this book; the Falk School of Sustainability and Environment for their continued support of interdisciplinary projects involving sustainability; and Michigan State University. We would not be able to include compelling information about companies already pushing the sustainability performance frontier if it were not for the many local and national companies and organizations that provided insight and examples for this book. Therefore, we need to thank 3M, Applied Products, Alcoa, Baxter, Bayer Material Sciences, Dow, DuPont, EMC, FedEx, Ford, GaBi, Global Reporting Initiative, General Motors, Herman Miller, Highmark, H. J. Heinz, Honeywell, IBM, Johnson & Johnson, Office Depot, Procter & Gamble, PITT OHIO, UPMC, Wesco, and Westinghouse. Finally, we would like to thank our families for supporting us and enabling the development of this book. To our children, we hope you will someday live in a sustainable world. To this book's readers, we hope you will spearhead the changes that make it possible for our children and all future generations to live in a sustainable world.

PART 1

Introduction to Strategic Sustainable Supply Chain Management (S³CM)

CHAPTER 1

Strategic Sustainable Supply Chain Management (S³CM)—The Next Industrial Revolution

Firms Map New Routes to Improved Profits and Sustainable Performance

Sustainability is viewed as "environmental, economic, and social well-being for today and tomorrow."
—International Institute for Sustainable Development[1]

Preface to the 3rd Edition

When the first edition of this book series was written, sustainable supply chains were very much of a new development. Consequently, their presence was surrounded by a great deal of confusion, dread, uncertainty, and misunderstanding. The first edition was intended to clarify what a sustainable supply chain was, why it was emerging, some of the dangers (and pitfalls) associated with sustainable supply chain management (SSCM), and the economic and marketing benefits of such supply chains. Since then, a great deal has changed. Consider, for a moment, the following changes that have taken place.

Sustainability Has Transitioned From a Minor Business/Strategic Issue to a Mainstream Issue

Sustainability is no longer something that is offered by certain firms (e.g., Unilever); it has been embraced by many traditional companies.

For example, Française de l'Energie (DDE)—a major French energy company—has become a leader in low carbon footprint energy production and recovery sites. Companies such as Heineken, Southwest Airlines, Phillips, and Nestlé publish a combined financial and sustainability report annually. Patagonia has set a high standard for sustainability in the fashion industry using sustainable materials, that is, recycled polyester, organic cotton, and fair labor practices in its supply chain along with more transparency and disclosure of information about its supply chain to the public. Increasingly, sustainability has become strategic in nature.

Sustainability Has Broadened Its Scope Beyond Pollution Prevention

For many readers and managers, sustainability was synonymous with pollution reduction and waste management. In other words, sustainability and the planet were one and the same. Over time, we have seen a broadening of this focus. Sustainability now includes issues such as corporate social responsibility (CSR), diversity, equity, and inclusion (DEI), and social and environmental justice issues. We now realize that sustainability that focuses on the planet only is not enough, if it does not include the other dimensions of performance.

Sustainability Is a Strategic Issue

In the first edition, we spent a great deal of time differentiating between the three approaches to sustainability—sustainability as public relations (SPR), sustainability as waste/cost minimization (SWM), and sustainability as corporate strategy (SCS). Increasingly, firms have recognized the limitations of the prior two approaches. Managers have come to realize that sustainability can form the basis of an effective strategy for differentiation and competing in an increasingly dynamic, diverse, turbulent marketplace. To illustrate this point, consider the following corporate examples:

- Salt + umber (www.saltandumber.com)—luxury fashion products.
- Cadbury—has launched a line of Vegan brand chocolates in the United Kingdom and reduced packaging waste in its candies through sugar cane packaging.
- H&M Group—fast fashion clothing—introduced a line of circular products that are made to last, and manufactured from safe, recycled, and sustainably sourced materials that can be repaired, reused, and remade many times. Supported by circular supply chains.
- Sunday Lawn Care—lawn care products—has designed and delivered a line of sustainable lawn care products that do not rely on polluting chemicals and fertilizers.

The striking issue about these examples is the breadth of product offerings—from fashion goods to lawn care. Senior executives are now recognizing that sustainability is an opportunity that differentiates firms in the marketplace, affects multiple products, and appeals to a diversity of consumers. It has become seen as forming a viable, effective corporate strategy.

Pressure for Improving Sustainability Is Coming From Numerous External Sources—The Consumer, Investment Groups, and the Government

Even if you decide that you do not want to compete on sustainability strategically, you cannot ignore these external pressures. Consider, for example, the experiences of Canada or the European Union, where sustainability has significantly influenced government policy.

Sustainability Has Been Adopted and Embraced by a Wide Range of Firms

Previously, sustainability had been embraced by certain "niche" firms. That has changed. Sustainability is now widely embraced by large firms (i.e., firms with 500 or more employees) and by small firms (i.e., firms with fewer than 500 employees). It has been embraced by international firms (e.g., WalMart and Unilever), Benefit Corporations such as The Body Shop, and by governmental agencies (e.g., the American Department of Defense). It has been embraced by small establishments such as Bell's Eccentric Café of Kalamazoo, MI (where diners are informed of the source of everything that they consume).

Sustainability Has Moved Beyond Reporting Requirements and Compliance

Initially, firms have sought to enforce this focus on sustainability by mandating compliance with certain appropriate standards (e.g., ISO 14001) or certain reporting requirements. We are now coming to realize that such an approach is fundamentally flawed. It is flawed for two reasons. First, compliance does not necessarily prove that a firm is sustainable or using sustainable approaches. Second, this approach targets the first tier. We now realize that to succeed with sustainability, we must go beyond the first tier. That is, it must involve the participation of the second, third, and fourth tiers. Yet, this realization has brought with it an awareness of the inherent challenges. Effective strategic sustainable supply chain management (S^3CM) requires investments by these lower-tier suppliers. Yet, there is a challenge that must be addressed and one that this revised book deals with—sustainability is an example of what is now being referred to as *Supply Chain Shaping Initiatives* (SCSI)—this type of supply chain initiative will be subsequently developed in greater detail. These are initiatives that shape the business environment and context in which supply chain activities take place; SCSIs seek values that drive the actions of individual supply chain partners. SCSIs often require the supply chain partners to make investments that most directly impact the target firms. This means that effective S^3CM requires firms to consider issues such as the state of buyer–supplier relationships and whether they (the focal firm) are considered to be "good" customers.

In other words, strategic supply chain management has continued to grow, develop, and evolve. This revised S^3CM series has been updated

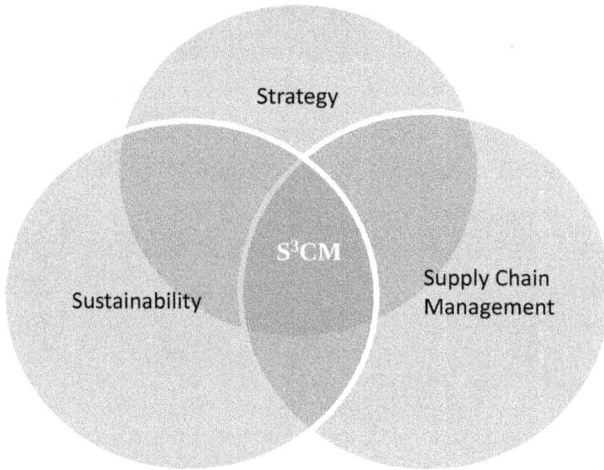

Figure 1.1 S³CM—foundations

to reflect these developments and to build on them. One of the first changes introduced involves how we view S³CM.

Strategic Sustainable Supply Chain Management— S³CM

One of this revised series's first notable features is the change in titles. This is not simply a marketing ploy but a repositioning of both the concept and the book. We are now bringing together three important developments/opportunities: strategy, sustainability, and the supply chain. Each development brings with it certain strengths and capabilities. What S³CM strives to do is to build on these capabilities and their interactions, resulting in a more powerful and holistic approach to this topic. This approach is captured in Figure 1.1. Note that S³CM lies at the interaction of the three developments.

Objectives

1. Define what S³CM is and is not.

2. Introduce the paradigm shift of sustainability, which does not involve dichotomous trade-offs but inclusive, collaborative, and integrative processes for improved performance.
3. Provide an evidence-based approach to show how developments over the last decade continue accelerating and impacting supply chain management.
4. Recognize that sustainability is not someone else's job, it's everyone's job!

S³CM—Will It Help Business?

It would be useful to start with the definition of a supply chain. It is the sum of a firm's customer relationships, order fulfillment, and supplier relationship processes, as well as the interconnected linkages among the suppliers of services, materials, information, and the customers of the firm's services or products. Supply chain managers are the people at various levels of an organization who are responsible for managing supply and demand, both within and across business organizations. There is a new collaborative opportunity for supply chain managers, and all business professionals, including a growing number of sustainability professionals, to work together on new dynamic business opportunities. For over a decade, there is substantial evidence of companies already solving existing business problems and proactively measuring and managing new profitable market segments.[2] The results of these collaborative efforts are competitive advantages through differentiated products and services for some, and resource efficiency for all.

These books aim to help you understand processes and improve performance. How? Management professionals need measurement tools and models to understand the current state of operations. This understanding informs decision-making and helps to identify strategic opportunities arising from measuring new performance metrics, sustainability reporting, and increasing levels of transparency. Why? Insights from McKinsey's Global survey results[3] from over 2,900 respondents (Figure 1.2) show that the integration of sustainability is widespread into processes ranging from mission and values, culture, operations, and strategic planning to employee engagement.

Interestingly, this study is from over a decade ago, and supply *chain management and budgeting lag behind other areas* of integration. There is ample room for supply chain management to close this integration gap. More recently, GlobeScan found that 67 percent of over 200 senior professionals in finance, technology, and sustainability functions believe sustainability is very important to commercial success. Yet, only 37 percent say sustainability is fully integrated into the core of business.[4] Companies are finding supply chains hold the key to unlocking reduced environmental impacts, energy conservation, community connected-ness, and performance improvements that have been overlooked until the paradigm shift of sustainability. Yet, it seems we are just getting started.

Supply chain and logistics analysts, procurement personnel, sustainability coordinators, managers, and executives face new pressures from their customers and from regulations to avoid social issues, reduce carbon emissions, and run more efficient and sustainable supply chains. Although the impression persists in many managers that implementing sustainable technologies or processes will be costly, our own research and

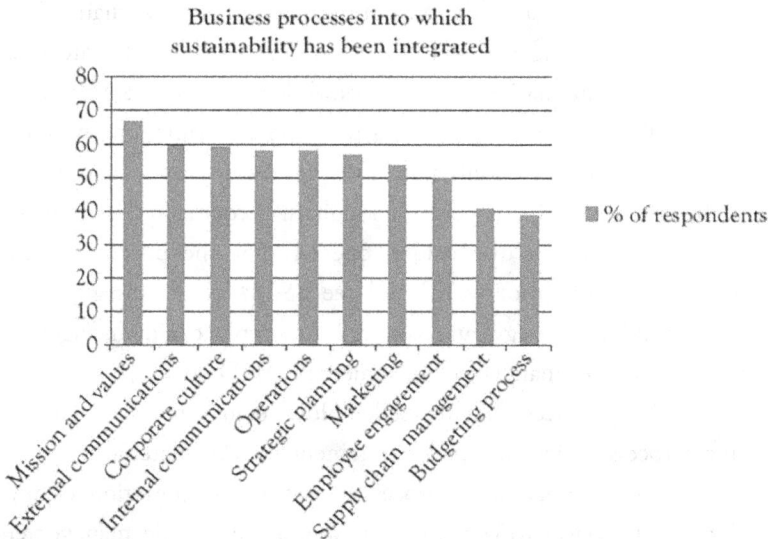

Figure 1.2 **Widespread integration**

the research of well-known consultancies and leading scholars suggest that trade-offs between costs and sustainability are a false dichotomy. We have now reached a tipping point where the benefits of not polluting outweigh the cost of creating pollution in the first place. Companies that focus on and implement sustainability programs outperform their industry averages in terms of profitability.

What is sustainability? At the time of writing this book, a Google search for "sustainable development" would yield over 91 million hits. If you searched more broadly for "sustainability," you would find over 185 million hits. The amount of information can be overwhelming, and we have heard some say that it's like drinking from a fire hose. A common thread to almost all definitions used by multinational companies includes the United Nations 1987 Brundtland Commission report "Our Common Future," which defined sustainable development as "meeting the needs of a current generation without compromising the needs of future generations." With a growing focus on sustainable development and the transition to a sustainable society, all definitions of sustainable development require that we, as decision-makers, see the world as a system—a system that connects space, time, and socioecological resources. What does this mean for the supply chain? Prior definitions recognizing the evolution of S³CM purposefully integrated the functions of purchasing and logistics while directing attention to the "green" attributes of processes with a focus on environmental performance. While this repositioning of the profession was a step in the right direction, it did not go far enough in recognizing the dynamic systems in which you, the reader, operate. For the purpose of this book, we build off prior work[5] and see *SSCM* as the integration of systems thinking, strategy, and action into supply chain management that must include financial, environmental, AND social performance. These S³CM practices include stakeholder engagement, materiality, product/process design, life-cycle assessment (LCA), materials selection and sourcing, manufacturing processes, waste, transportation of final products and services to consumers as well as end-of-life management of products, and closed-loop systems. An important new element of SSCM is the integration of systems thinking (the holistic approach to

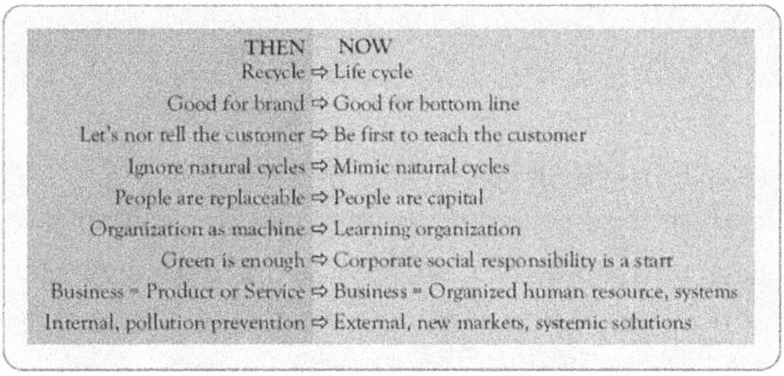

THEN   NOW
Recycle ⇨ Life cycle
Good for brand ⇨ Good for bottom line
Let's not tell the customer ⇨ Be first to teach the customer
Ignore natural cycles ⇨ Mimic natural cycles
People are replaceable ⇨ People are capital
Organization as machine ⇨ Learning organization
Green is enough ⇨ Corporate social responsibility is a start
Business = Product or Service ⇨ Business = Organized human resource, systems
Internal, pollution prevention ⇨ External, new markets, systemic solutions

Figure 1.3 Sustainability: Then versus now

analysis focusing on the way that a system's constituent parts interrelate and how systems work over time and within the context of larger systems).[6] By including and starting with a systems understanding, we can define success and align with and enable strategic planning, while assessing multiple actions with analysis supported by standards and tools. This approach to S³CM and a framework for strategic sustainable development[7] enables any organization to recognize new sustainability opportunities as we transition to a more sustainable society. The foundations of S³CM will be covered in more detail both in this book (Volume 1) and in Volume 2 on implementation. In both volumes, we take an evidence-based approach to enable sustainability's full potential in managing supply chains.

S³CM highlights an important aspect of the transition of the supply chain management concept (Figure 1.3). Sustainability is not simply environmental sustainability but corporate sustainability, and something John Elkington coined in 1997 as the "triple bottom line" approach to the measurement and management of all value created and impacts upon financial, environmental, AND social systems performance. We take this a step further and propose that sustainability provides integrated bottom line (IBL) benefits.[8]

What Is Sustainable? Outdated notions of the "green corporation" are being replaced by a new model: the learning organization that rethinks products, processes, and corporate culture to unleash game-changing innovation making better use of

socioecological resources while solving global systemic problems.[*]

Defining the concept is a good starting point for providing a
context in which businesses and managers can envision this fast-moving
paradigm. A definition by itself will not do much for an organization as
a critical part of the process of developing a definition is to realize that
sustainability is in itself, the end goal. To realistically operationalize any
vision, there is growing evidence that sustainability is the new foundation for innovation and strategic competition. This evidence will allow
many firms to cross a chasm that separates the innovators and early
adopters from the rest while continuously improving business processes
and supply chains.

Our own research over the past 15 years and recent work
with sustainability and supply chain executives have uncovered many
hidden opportunities surrounding the integration of sustainability
into operations and supply chains. There is overwhelming evidence
of organizations achieving both high customer service and cost-effectiveness while also successfully integrating sustainability throughout
their processes. To this end, Accenture,[9] worked with 245 supply
chain executives to identify high-performing organizations as those
who achieved top quartile performance on both cost-effectiveness and
customer service, while laggards occupied the lower quartile. The
high-performing firms take practical and cost-effective steps to address
their environmental impact. They are not just looking at only the
important "last mile" of distribution but are also taking an integrated view through their entire supply chain (Figure 1.4). The research
suggests that high-performing firms are:

- Designing products while working across business functions
  to integrating sustainability within the product development
  processes.

---

[*]The integration of sustainability can be found within business schools internationally and the realization that future managers need to recognize and
differentiate perceptions, myths, and facts surrounding this paradigm. Figure
created by Diane Ramos.

Research and
development

Closed-loop
systems

Sourcing and
procurement

Changing customer
expectations
integrated into
decision making

End-of-life,
cradle to cradle

Manufacturing

Sustainability integrated
across the product
life cycle

Consumption

Distrubution
and selling

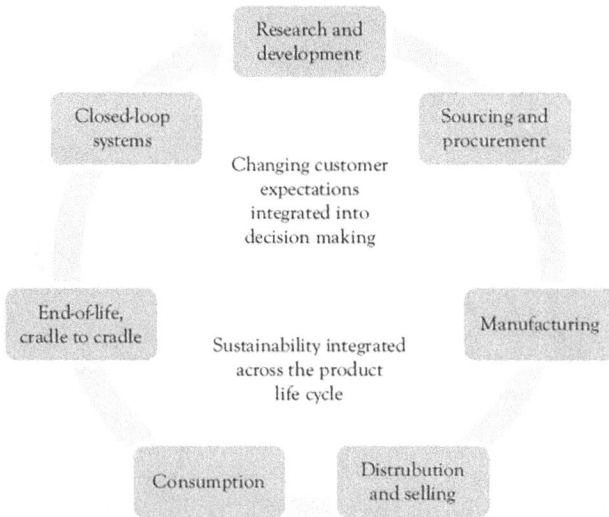

Figure 1.4 Integrated view of supply chain management

- Actively working with suppliers to lower their supply chain carbon footprint.
- Seeking the most practical solutions to their most material sustainability challenges.
- Choosing systems and processes investments that offer the best possible return while also considering environmental impacts.
- Creating value from the integration of sustainability across business functions and the supply chain.

These same firms recognize that now is the time to act on sustainability.

Innovative firms are creating more sustainable and high-performing supply chains by integrating and collaborating across three performance measures to drive value: cost efficiency, service quality, AND sustainability. Integrating all three measures creates opportunities for profit improvement, through operating cost reduction and cash flow improvement. This integrated approach aligns with strategic opportunities by linking investments in customer service with more sustainable business practices. Where a traditional business case would only look for the best balance between cost-effectiveness and quality of service over the

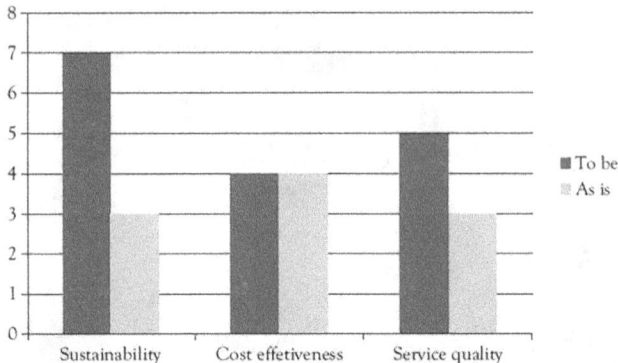

Figure 1.5 **A multidimensional approach to business supply chain opportunities**

lifetime of the investment, Accenture suggests that top-performing firms are increasingly likely to develop a more sophisticated, three-dimensional business case to assess the value of supply chain projects[10] (Figure 1.5). Here, the value added or return on investment is better clarified by considering the likelihood of measuring sustainability improvement from a project, in addition to the cost and service implications.

The influence of sustainability on corporate behavior and performance outcomes is growing.[11] A comparison of firms that voluntarily adopted environmental and social policies years ago exhibited fundamentally different characteristics from a matched sample of firms that adopted almost none of these policies. Researchers from Harvard found that the boards of directors of the adopting firms are more likely to be responsible for sustainability if incentives to top executives are linked to sustainability metrics. Moreover, adopting firms are more likely to have organized procedures for stakeholder engagement, to be more long-term oriented, and to exhibit more measurement and disclosure of nonfinancial information. In addition, they found that adopting firms significantly outperform their counterparts over the long term, regarding both stock market and accounting performance. This performance is stronger in sectors where the customers are individual end consumers Business to Consumer (B2C), compared to Business to Business (B2B) companies that compete on the basis of brand and reputation, and when products significantly depend on extracting large amounts of natural resources.

Foundations of Sustainability

A system's approach to sustainability builds on certain fundamental premises, as summarized in Table 1.1. This approach encompasses a holistic and modular view of business processes synthesizing knowledge about the parts into understanding the whole. When allowed to look at supply chains in this way, we can better grasp the entire system and its many details and change focus when needed to view different levels so that we are not overwhelmed by its overall complexity. As you will see throughout the following chapters, this approach helps to reduce risk while improving performance so that the effects of waste or unforeseen problems can be confined within a subsystem, preventing systemwide collapse. These premises form the foundation of successful, effective sustainability through the supply chain. Each element contributes to the creation of value and success of a supply chain.

Sustainability focuses on the 3Ps—product/process/packaging. Supply chain sustainability involves focusing on three elements: product (primarily its design), process (how the items are made and delivered), and packaging (how the items are protected for storage and delivery). If these are managed in terms of their environmental impact, then the firm can significantly reduce its overall sustainability footprint.

Product design. Here, we look at issues such as the material used (type and quantity), the ease with which the product can be disassembled, and the ease with which it can be recycled and whether we are dealing with recycling, downcycling, or upcycling. Introduced by McDonough and Braungart (2002),[12] downcycling is when an item is recycled into a usable but lower-grade product that does not eliminate the initial need for the original product. White office paper is a good example of downcycling. When we use white, bright paper and put it in a recycle bin, the paper can be transformed into paper that is not quite as bright. Alternatively, upcycling[13] happens when a product is reused as an input to a product of a higher quality or value than the original,

Table 1.1 *Foundations of sustainable supply chain management*

- Focus on the 3Ps—product/process/packaging
- Prevention is preferred to correction
- Sustainability is integrated into the day-to-day life of the firm
- Sustainability is captured within strategic, tactical, and operational performance
- Sustainability is a system opportunity
- Sustainability must be linked to the strategy and the bottom line
- Value propositions include environmental and social performance
- Waste is a symptom, not the root cause
- Waste is ultimately linked to processes
- Waste elimination and management are economically driven

moving resources back up the supply chain. An example could be used newspaper crafted into ballet flats (shoes).

The importance of product design should never be underestimated. Experience has shown that product design, while not expensive overall, greatly impacts the ultimate performance of the product. Statistics often cited for the importance of product design include: (1) its influence on up to 70 to 80 percent of the resulting product costs; and (2) changes that can be made quickly and easily in product design could cost far more if made at later stages. Some have referred to this second statistic as the 1–10–100 rule, where a design change that would cost $1 to make during the design phase would cost $10 to make during prototyping and $100 to make during production.

To apply the lessons that we have learned from total quality management (TQM) to sustainability, we can say sustainability always begins with good product design.

Process. Here, we focus on how the product is made—the processes involved in making and delivering the product. We should look not only at how the product is made within our firm but also within the systems of our suppliers. We look at the costs associated with transporting products from our suppliers. Our goal is to identify the waste created within this production process over the entire supply chain and understand how to significantly reduce it.

Packaging. Packaging is created to protect the product from damage, enable more efficient packing of transport (to reduce the amount of space left unused and to protect the product), and facilitate its display. The problem with packaging is that once it has fulfilled these needs, it is often thrown away, increasing the product's environmental impact. By focusing on packaging materials, we look at the challenges of meeting the needs of packaging while (1) reducing the amount of packaging used; (2) ensuring that the packaging material is part of closed-loop systems using recycled material; and (3) ensuring that the packaging itself can be reduced. The following experiences of Dell and In.gredient show that packaging offers many opportunities for sustainability.

Dell is focusing on both revolutionizing and simplifying computer packages. At the heart of this program launched years ago is a focus on the three Cs—(1) Cube (what is the size of the box and can it be smaller); (2) Content (what is the packaging material made of and can it be made of something better); and (3) Curb (can the packaging material be easily recycled). Since the start of this program, Dell has shrunk packaging volume by 10 percent, increased the amount of recycled content by 45 percent, and increased recycled packaging material by 75 percent.

In.gredient, a grocery store in Austin, Texas, is focusing on engaging customers to reduce waste. The store was designed to reduce packaging waste by eliminating packaging. Customers are encouraged to bring their own containers to pack up items such as grains, oils, and dairy. If a customer does not have a container, In.gredient will sell them a compostable container. The founders of In.gredient hope that this approach will make a significant impact on the level of waste created in grocery stores. Consider the following:

- Americans add over 570 million pounds of food packaging to their landfills every day.
- Getting food to our tables eats up 10 percent of the U.S. total energy budget.
- Prepackaged food forces consumers to buy more than they need, stuffing both their stomachs and landfills.

- Approximately 40 percent of the food brought into U.S. kitchens is thrown away after traveling over 1,500 miles to get to us.

Prevention is preferred to correction. When dealing with the problems created by the lack of sustainability (e.g., excess pollution, employee unrest), we are faced with two options. The first is that we can focus on and treat the effects. If pollutants are too high, we install scrubbers to catch the particulates and prevent them from getting into the air. In the short term, this approach can be effective. However, in the long term, it is doomed to fail because the processes that caused the problems continue to operate; the pollution (waste) is still being created. Over the long term, the costs, direct and indirect, hidden and obvious, continue to accumulate. Ultimately, managers must realize that the only effective long-term solution is to prevent the problems from being created in the first place. Thus, our second option is to uncover the reasons for the problems and attack those reasons directly.

Sustainability is integrated into the day-to-day life of the firm. In many ways, experiences with sustainability parallel the firm's experiences with TQM. One of the major lessons of TQM was that quality could never be improved if the responsibility for quality was separated from the day-to-day life of the firm and its employees and assigned to a separate department. This approach created a situation where those responsible for quality problems were not held accountable for improving quality— a situation that management found to be untenable in the long term. Similarly, when it comes to sustainability, we can see that sustainability works best when it is integrated into the daily lives of the employees; those who create problems with sustainability are also held accountable for generating the solutions that can reduce these problems.

Sustainability is captured within corporate performance measurement. Performance measures play an important role in the life of every firm and supply chain. In many ways, the performance measurement and management system (PMMS) plays a role in the firm similar to the body's nervous system. The PMMS, like the central nervous system, is both a control and a communication system. It is a control in that we measure performance, compare that level of performance to a standard, and take appropriate corrective action. More importantly, the PMMSs are communication tools. The PMMS communicates what is important by the simple action of measurement. If we measure something, then we are telling everyone within and outside of an organization that it is important. Alternatively, if we do not measure something, then the message to the firm is that it is not important.

For measures to act effectively as communication, they must be *meaningful*. That is, they must make sense to the various levels involved. Metrics reported to top management are not necessarily reported in the same way to the employees working on the shop floor. People working on the floor think in terms of units made, lead time, or reject rates; top management views activities in terms of sales, profits, gross margins, and return on assets. Consequently, measures must communicate with these various groups using different terms.

Finally, we should also recognize that measures can be used to develop a scorecard—to show where we are doing well in terms of sustainability and where further improvement is needed. We will drill down deeper into sustainability measures later in Chapters 5 and 6.

Sustainability is a systems opportunity. We must recognize that problems with sustainability are not the sole responsibility of any one group or area. After all, opportunities with sustainability arise from the actions taken by many different groups in the firm:

- Purchasing (how they manage the purchasing process, the type of suppliers they buy from, how they evaluate supplier performance, and how they develop potential suppliers).
- Engineering (how products and processes are designed).
- Accounting and Finance (how performance is measured and communicated; how costs are captured and future value assessed).
- Logistics (how products are shipped and how the costs of shipping are determined).
- Manufacturing (how the processes are managed and controlled).
- Organizational behavior (how people are recruited and trained, the type of people we have in the system).

- Top management (determining what is important and the role played by strategic sustainability in the future of the firm).

Because many employees are responsible for impacting sustainability performance, it is critical that they should be involved in its management. Just like a cross-functional team is most effective for product design, so too is a cross-functional team most appropriate for sustainability. Furthermore, in many cases, this team should involve representatives from the supplier and the customer sides of the business. We should recognize that sustainability is an "opportunity." When an issue involving sustainability occurs, we have a chance to understand what contributed to that issue (symptom) and to correct the underlying root cause (the actual problem) once and for all.

Sustainability only works if it is something that everyone thinks about every day. That only occurs if it is integrated. If we think back to Union Carbide, prior to the Bhopal India disaster, they were often viewed as a leader in many business performance metrics. Yet internally, environmental compliance was looked at as some other department's responsibility, as this was a separate function. If environmental risks are ignored, these risks will only be reviewed after there is a problem. Sometimes, this manifests as a fine from the government, other times it can lead to an accident (Bhopal, India—December 1984) with more than 3,000 dying within weeks and over 8,000 since killed from gas-related diseases. A governmental affidavit issued in 2006 claimed that the incident caused 558,125 injuries including 38,470 temporal and partially disabling injuries. The impact on this firm was significant and a postmortem revealed a lack of integration of environmental compliance into day-to-day operations, that most of the safety systems were in poor condition, and that tanks were overfilled. Ultimately, a runaway reaction caused a tank rupture releasing a large volume of toxic gas. Workers did not know that they should not clean pipes with water and may have helped to cause the problem.

Value propositions include environmental and social performance. As shown in prior examples of companies already measuring, managing, and reporting sustainability issues, that is, environmental, social, and governance performance. Annual sustainability reporting, the Security

Exchange Commission (SEC) filing asking for a description and protocol used to report greenhouse gas (GHG) emissions,[14] and corporate goals of carbon neutrality all signal a changing license to operate and value proposition for firms. This evolving value proposition needs to be translated to customer understanding.

Waste is a symptom, not the root cause. Waste is anything that does not add value to a product or service. Raw materials have a first cost in their acquisition, yet other unintended costs in process inefficiencies. Waste in the form of pollution, that is GHGs, has additional costs to handle, track, and dispose of, and should be recognized as a process and supply chain inefficiency. Simply stated, pollution is a *symptom*—a quantitative indicator of a problem. It tells us that something has gone wrong; not why it has gone wrong. It tells us the magnitude of the problems; it does not show what factors have contributed. Pollution is equivalent to a thermometer—it shows improvements and decreases in performance. Yet, stop for a moment and think about the implications of placing a dollar value on pollution by metric ton, volume, or pound. How will this change process and SSCM as we look for new forms of efficiency and effectiveness during the next industrial revolution of waste elimination?

When dealing with symptoms, we must remember certain management "truths." First, we should think in terms of whole *systems* and never attack a symptom directly. If we attack symptoms, then we experience a "good news/bad news" situation. That is, in the short term, the symptoms experienced will decrease, only to reappear at the same place in the future or to appear in another place today. For example, we decide to attack the high level of particulates by installing a scrubber. The number of particulates emitted falls: the good news. We now have tons of captured particulates that must be safely and inexpensively disposed of: the bad news. The real opportunity is when the particulates can be sold as raw material input for another company and upcycled to become gypsum board, for example. Second, when we encounter a symptom, we must be prepared to take a step back, to understand the system and to identify the processes that are giving rise to these problems/symptoms.

Waste is ultimately linked to processes. One thing that we have learned from lean/just-in-time (JIT) systems is the importance of understanding the set of following relationships:

- Pollution is an output.
- Outputs are the results of processes.
- If you do not like the output, change the process.

In other words, to reduce pollution and improve sustainability, we must focus on the process that generates these outputs. It is only by changing the processes that we can develop true mastery over sustainability, waste management, and pollution elimination. It is also one reason that this book contains more than one chapter devoted to this topic.

Waste elimination and management are driven by economics. Some years ago, one of the authors was talking with Chrysler's Vice President (VP) of Environmental Affairs. In the conversation, the VP made a strong statement—he never encountered a well-thought-out environmental management proposal that failed to generate a positive return on investments. More importantly, he continued, this insight was good because it showed everyone in Chrysler that pollution reduction was not only good for the environment but also good for the bottom line. This is an important lesson. We must recognize that most managers are conservative and risk-adverse. They will invest in, and more importantly support, only those initiatives that are economically justifiable—that is, where the benefits exceed the costs. If a sustainability-oriented initiative is not economically viable, then it will be pursued only when (1) the law requires it or (2) it is the "right" thing to do. These conditions occur infrequently, and they are not likely to generate widespread support or enthusiasm for such initiatives.

In reality, the challenge of ensuring that pollution management is driven by economics requires management to take a total cost perspective, that is, management must consider not only direct cost saving (e.g., reduced material, energy, or labor costs) but also indirect costs (e.g., reduced floor space, fewer inspections, less sorting, fewer bills of material, less training, healthier and more productive employees) and the potential for increased revenue (due to the potential attractiveness and ability to differentiate the resulting products). These costs must consider not only cost savings but also cost avoidance (a more difficult concept to measure). This is why *life-cycle costing* is so critical, as we discuss in Chapters 5 and 6 of Volume 1.

Here are three issues to consider:[†]

- In most firms, the ratio between value-adding and nonvalue-adding activities (as measured in terms of both time and costs) is 1 to 1,000–2,000.
- In world-class firms, this same ratio is 1 to 200–300.
- According to the same Chrysler VP previously referenced, for every $1 saved in direct savings, typically $6 is saved in indirect costs.

This emphasis on economic justification forces managers to view sustainability not as a moral imperative, but as an investment in financial, natural, AND ultimately human capital.

Sustainability must be linked to the strategy and the bottom line. Ultimately, for sustainability to be integrated within a firm, it must be first embraced by top management. Top management is widely recognized as critical for the success of any management/corporate initiative. Every textbook or management text that deals with such developments as TQM or JIT/lean always emphasizes the need for top management involvement and commitment. Top management's involvement and public support lend credibility to management/corporate initiatives. When top management is involved, then necessary resources can be devoted to the initiative. When top management is involved, everyone in the firm knows that the initiative is important and that it must be supported.

Yet, to secure this support, we have to show top management that in supporting the initiative, they also help themselves. This occurs most clearly when we can link the sustainability initiative to the strategy or the bottom line. In the previous point, we talked about the linkages to the bottom line; however, the linkage to the corporate strategy is even

---

[†]Based on the experiences of the authors.

more important. A good example can be found in Dell Computing's approach to its environmental initiatives.

Dell has introduced a wide range of sustainability initiatives, including the following:

- *Dell Ecovative Design for Packaging.* Dell introduced a new kind of innovative mushroom-based packaging created by Ecovative Design. This new packaging reduced the total amount of solid waste and consumption of fossil fuels. It is made from completely compostable material and only takes one-tenth of the total time to produce, unlike styrofoam.
- *Dell India Green Initiative.* Dell India sends out a coupon to encourage recycling of computers. If you send in old Dell Systems to Dell for recycling, you receive a special discount for your next Dell computer purchase. Then there is the Dell Go Green Challenge. This challenge raises community awareness and involvement in green projects throughout India.
- *Recycling for Home and Business Initiatives.* Dell offers an extensive recycling program for its home and business customers. Dell has partnered with FedEx to provide an at-home product pickup program. For business users, this program is especially attractive as Dell will assume responsibility for any subsequent disposal issues. Hard disks, for example, are overwritten and destroyed using military-specified procedures. The program is absolutely free and can be used for any Dell products as well as non-Dell products, if the customer purchases a similar type of product from Dell. This program has enabled Dell to differentiate itself from competitors such as Apple, Lenovo, or Hewlett-Packard. It has generated a great deal of positive visibility for Dell.

When such initiatives are linked to corporate strategy, we take a step to the "AND" paradigm discussed at the beginning of this chapter. When sustainability and corporate strategy are linked, then top management knows that they are not forced to make trade-offs between profit/strategic advantage and improved sustainability.

Summary and Next Steps

This chapter started by answering the question, "Will sustainability help business?" The overwhelming response to this is "yes," across multiple dimensions of performance and value creation while reducing negative impacts on the environment and society.

More dimensions of sustainability will be explored in the remaining foundational chapters of Volume 1, and Volume 2 will extend this into implementation. By reading this book and purposefully setting aside some of your time to gain insight from a series of action items (AIs) found within each chapter, the end goal of this process should be a tailored approach to supply chain transformation. This transformation starts with understanding sustainable supply chains and their benefits before we systematically assess our own supply chain to help identify and execute sustainable practices. The assessment process presented in these volumes will help develop a sustainable supply chain vision and strategy: create an executable plan for new sustainable supply chain projects; provide opportunities to integrate sustainable practices throughout your company, as well as among suppliers and customers; bring about better clarity regarding supply chain processes; leverage existing enterprise-resource-planning (ERP)-enabled manufacturing activities (energy consumption, emissions, scrap and waste, recycling, remanufacturing, and packaging); help guide you as to where to look for improvements in warehousing and fleet management; enable strategic sourcing highlighting the importance of design thinking, programs for sustainable raw materials and packaging; and how to plan for closed-loop systems and reverse logistics activities, while leveraging existing systems and programs to identify and operationalize opportunities for existing and new sustainability practices.

Information within this book is sequenced to help accomplish all of the aforementioned while taking the complex paradigm of sustainability and breaking it down into constituent parts focusing on how systems work. Chapters begin with evidence-based management, highlighting short vignettes, recent trends, and sustainability initiatives from innovative and early adopting firms. Information within chapters reveals applicable frameworks, tools, and proven standards as enablers of SSCM initiatives. The end of each chapter challenges readers to reflect on their own operations through applied action-learning opportunities focusing the reader on AIs.

Applied Learning: Action Items—Steps You Can Take to Apply the Learning From This Chapter

AI: Look for a definition of sustainability from a competitor and reflect on how this can be improved upon and aligned within your own firm.

AI: What are the environmental and social impacts of your supply chain?

AI: To what extent can you impact the 3Ps to eliminate waste?

AI: What are the three most important trends in your industry?

AI: How rapid or intense are each of the following in your industry: changes in marketing, rate of product or service obsolesce, actions of competitors, and changes in production/service technology?

Further Readings

Lubin, D. and D. Esty. "The Sustainability Imperative." *Harvard Business Review* 8, no. 5 (2010): 43–50.

McDonough, W., M. Braungart, and B. Clinton. *The Upcycle: Beyond Sustainability—Designing for Abundance*. Macmillan, 2013.

Porter, M. E. and M. R. Kramer. "The Big Idea: Creating Shared Value, Rethinking Capitalism." *Harvard Business Review* 89, no. 1/2 (2011): 62–77.

Meadows and Wright. 2018. *Thinking in Systems: A Primer, Sustainability Institute.*

Villena, V. and D. Gioia. "A More Sustainable Supply Chain." *Harvard Business Review* 98, no. 2 (2020): 84–93.

Zimon, D., J. Tyan, and R. Sroufe. "Drivers of Sustainable Supply Chain Management: Practices to Alignment With un Sustainable Development goals." *International Journal for Quality Research* 14, no. 1 (2020).

CHAPTER 2

Strategic Sustainability—Systems Integration and Planning

We can't impose our will on a system. We can listen to what the system tells us, and discover how its properties and our values can work together to bring forth something much better than could ever be produced by our will alone.

—Donella H. Meadows

What Happens When We Plan for Integration?

- The parent company of toy manufacturer, Lego, has invested in one of Germany's largest offshore wind farms with over 160 megawatts of renewable energy—a move to bolster the firm's energy consumption with goals of 100 percent renewables was completed in 2017, three years ahead of schedule, with additional goals including a carbon neutral supply chain.

- Praxair, a global Fortune 300 company that supplies atmospheric, process and specialty gases, high-performance coatings, and related services, voluntarily began collecting environmental key performance indicators (KPIs) in productivity projects. In one year, 8 percent of Praxair projects were tagged "sustainable development" and produced $32 million and 278,000 metric tons of carbon dioxide (CO_2) equivalent in savings.

- Starbucks has used Coffee and Farmer Equity (C.A.F.E.) Practices—a set of guidelines to achieve product quality, social responsibility, economic accountability, and environmental leadership. Their annual report maps these practices into the

United Nations Sustainable Development Goals (UN SDGs).
They have even offered sustainability bonds to support sustainable coffee sourcing and leading efforts for positive environmental
and social impacts on global coffee supply chains.

We next extend the definition of S^3CM within the larger context of
systems stressing the integration of environmental, social, and governance (ESG) performance measurement and management throughout a
product's life cycle. When defining the S^3CM concept, we are introducing
a paradigm shift of sustainability as not involving dichotomous trade-offs
but as an inclusive, collaborative, and integrating process for improved
performance. The abovementioned vignettes are not explicitly about
logistics. However, the actions of Lego, Praxair, and Starbucks have supply
chain impacts involving inputs to systems such as energy, the importance
of measurement, and new social sustainability efforts up and down a
supply chain. By the end of this chapter, you will see that sustainability
is not someone else's job but an opportunity for *everyone* to improve
products and processes, utilize cleaner energy sources, and simultaneously
reduce missions across multiple evolving performance dimensions with an
integrated supply chain management approach.

Objectives

1. Review trends impacting the future of S^3CM.
2. See how S^3CM needs systems integration as it becomes more
   sustainable.
3. See sustainability as a strategic initiative with an applied
   approach to planning for it.

Risks of Waiting: Compliance Is Not Enough

Adverse weather conditions, polycrisis (e.g., where multiple crises
intertwine, their causes and processes inextricably bound together to
create compounded effects), wars, commodity volatility, and a range
of threats have been very visible in recent years. These disruptions are
only growing more frequent. Hurricanes, wildfires, droughts, and deep

freezes are costly and deadly. In the United States, we are experiencing 20 weather disasters each year, with over a billion in economic losses, compared to an average of 7.4 annual billion-dollar disasters since 1980.[1] Despite the measures taken to combat these events, the sentiment among procurement executives is that weather-related events will only continue to increase costs. The Procurement Intelligence Unit[2] estimated over a decade ago that the Forbes Global 2000 stands to lose a staggering €280 billion from weather-related events. They were on the right track, as we found that natural disasters worldwide caused around $280 billion in economic losses in 2021, up from $210 billion in 2020 and $166 billion in 2019. The Procurement Intelligence Unit research, which took into account the views of 181 senior procurement executives, also showed that the procedures aimed at reducing the impact of unexpected events are limited. Most businesses assume that suppliers will take responsibility for managing supply continuity, with a minority of firms actively deploying strategies that extend to suppliers' suppliers. There exists a critical opportunity for systems thinking, systems integration, and better supply chain planning for an uncertain future.

There is growing evidence of businesses taking practical actions to embed sustainability within their day-to-day supply chain operations.[*] The vignettes at the start of this chapter highlight companies and some results, but what is most needed is a vision and planning process for integrating sustainability into S^3CM. This vision starts with an understanding and an integrated view of the entire supply chain from raw material extraction to disposal or opportunities for closed-loop, cradle-to-cradle (C2C) systems. The vision is supported by understanding the organization's current state, developing creative solutions, and prioritizing options. There is now a need to focus on the integration of performance measurement, embedding cost effectiveness, a focus on customer service and simultaneous sustainability improvement within the total cost of ownership. For example, when looking for new performance measures, start with carbon dioxide (CO_2) and look into other GHG emissions. Why carbon dioxide? There is already a price on it and several countries have trading platforms for CO_2. China has six trading platforms. As

---

[*]KPMG (2011a and b) with 378 senior executives surveyed.

previously mentioned, CO_2 represents waste from a process that adds no value to a product or process. Calculate the carbon footprint of your own operations and those of your supply chain and take steps to incrementally integrate CO_2 into the business case for projects with goals for CO_2 reduction. Finally, when making the business case for new sustainability projects, deploy the most cost-effective and proven technologies. Deploying your vision of sustainability requires a systematic approach. Those organizations that take the lead in developing innovative supply chain strategies and then proactively embed sustainability within their operations will be the most likely stay ahead on supply chain performance over the longer term. What is your vision?

Trends to Watch

Evidence of changing customer expectations and sustainability moving up the corporate agenda was confirmed by a KPMG global survey of senior executives,[3] which found the following:

- About 62 percent of firms surveyed have a strategy for corporate sustainability with 23 percent of firms in the process of developing a plan.
- Primary drivers for sustainability are resource- and energy-efficient, with brand enhancement, regulatory policy, and risk management still remaining key drivers.
- About 44 percent of executives in the study see sustainability as a source of innovation, whereas 39 percent see sustainability as a source of new business opportunity.
- Firms are increasingly measuring and reporting their sustainability performance and businesses want a successor to the Kyoto Protocol.
- About 67 percent of executives believe that a new set of rules is "very important" or "critical" to have a clear road map for sustainability with corporate-lobbying efforts pushing for tighter rules.

With increasing scrutiny of corporate carbon emissions, freight and transportation providers have every opportunity to strategically impact and realize sustainable value from their operations. Emissions from freight in the United States are projected to increase by 74 percent between 2005 and 2035. China is expected to increase its use of freight transportation fuels by 4.5 percent a year from 2008 to 2035. Global freight emissions are predicted to increase by 40 percent in the same period.[3] Given this growth, we paradoxically have significant influence over the carbon footprint of supply chain operations. Decisions on how products are designed and packaged, along with where products are made, store locations, offsetting, and how much time is allotted for transit, all impact GHG emissions and waste within business systems.[4] We should all have a strategy for corporate sustainability, its measurement, and how we will report our progress. Shippers will find cleaner and more cost-efficient freight practices and integrated systems with good returns on investment. Sustainability is a way to differentiate operations, improve brand loyalty, provide new services, and a road map for long-term goals.

With sights set on achieving more sustainable supply chains, objectives for some companies (e.g., the Consumer Goods Forum, HP, Microsoft, and others) include optimizing shared supply chains, engaging technologically savvy consumers, while also improving consumer health and well-being.[†] The ability to achieve these objectives is essential to the consumer goods industry. The difference between success and failure in this industry would be the ability to adapt to rapid and significant change.[5] The trends with the biggest influence on industry objectives for the next 10 years include the following:

1. Increased urbanization
2. Aging population
3. Increasing spread of wealth
4. Increasing impact of consumer technology adoption
5. Increase in consumer service demands
6. Increased importance of health and well-being

[†]2020 Future Value Chain Project.

7. Growing consumer concern about sustainability
8. Shifting of economic power
9. Scarcity of natural resources
10. Increase in regulatory pressure
11. Rapid adoption of supply chain technology capabilities
12. Impact of next-generation information technologies

Within the context of these trends, the industry needs a fundamental change in the integration of consumer products companies and retailer's business models for serving changing consumer needs. This means working collaboratively with industry, governments, nongovernmental organizations (NGOs), and consumers. The four primary objectives coming out of the study are (1) making business more sustainable, (2) optimizing a shared supply chain, (3) engaging with technology-enabled consumers, and (4) serving the health and well-being of consumers. Like the information technology and quality megatrends of the past, sustainability will touch every function, every business line, and every employee.[6] Companies that excel in sustainability shift their leadership, systematized use of tools, strategic alignment, integration, reporting, and communication. They move from tactical, ad hoc, and siloed approaches to strategic, systematic, and integrated practices.

Add to these trends the following recent events: the signing of the Climate Accord in Paris, release of the UN's 17 SDGs, toxic air in parts of China causing manufacturing to shut down or slow down, and the Pope's Laudato Si, a pandemic, Intergovernmental Panel on Climate Change (IPCC) reports, the SEC requiring disclosure of GHG emissions, and we need to ask ourselves a few questions. One, which new business leaders will emerge in this dynamic environment? Two, how will these leaders reorganize business as a vehicle for systemic change?

Systems Integration: A Foundation of Competition

There is now a shift in S³CM. Historically, we have seen price-driven yet strategically decoupled S³CM. The move for many is now value

driven *and* strategically coupled S³CM. We see an increasing emphasis on integrated and a more comprehensive set of outcomes, where
the integration draws on the following six outcomes: value, resilience,
responsiveness, security, sustainability, and innovation. As the language
of sustainability has evolved over time, so too will the ways in which
we measure performance. Environmental performance has given way
to sustainability, and innovation is yet another lens we can use to
see this evolving paradigm. To take this concept further, others are
extending sustainability to understanding and enabling the purpose of
corporations as creating "shared value"[7] not just profit. So what are we
getting at? Sustainability calls for the integration of systems like no other
business paradigm.

Why focus on sustainability beyond the firm to the supply chain?
Systems integration and the increasing importance of supply chains as
the basis of competition call for every business to go beyond its own
four walls to better measure, monitor, and manage sustainable supply
chains. The reality of managing supply chains is dynamic and requires
a concerted effort to align with new programs and opportunities, such
as sustainability. Ironically, the realities of managing supply chains are
the same as sustainability (i.e., visibility, control, risk, transparency,
complexity, and collaboration). Strategic sustainable development can
help organizations overcome the obstacles of paradigm change and
provide a new path toward the identification of opportunities and
planning. When looking at suppliers, some of you are willing to work
with for certifications and to generally help them. Others are key
suppliers and need higher levels of transparency, the application of
frameworks, and relationship building.

Framework for Strategic Sustainable Development

The Natural Step (TNS: www.naturalstep.org) is an organization
founded in Sweden in the late 1980s by scientist Karl-Henrik
Robèrt. Following publication of the Brundtland Report in 1987,
Robèrt developed TNS framework,[8] proposing four system conditions
for the sustainability of human activities on earth. Robèrt's system
conditions are derived from the laws of thermodynamics, promote

systems thinking, and set the foundation for how we can approach decision making.

The first and second laws of thermodynamics set limiting conditions for life on earth. The first law says that energy is conserved; nothing disappears, its form simply changes. The implications of the second law are that matter and energy tend to disperse over time. This is referred to as "entropy." Merging the two laws and applying them to life on earth, the following becomes apparent:

1. All the matter that will ever exist on earth is here now (first law).
2. Disorder increases in all closed systems and the Earth is a closed system with respect to matter (second law). However, it is an open system with respect to energy since it receives energy from the sun.
3. Sunlight is responsible for almost all increases in net material quality on the planet through photosynthesis and solar heating effects. Chloroplasts in plant cells take energy from sunlight for plant growth. Plants, in turn, provide energy for other forms of life, such as animals. Evaporation of water from the oceans by solar heating produces most of the Earth's fresh water. This flow of energy from the sun creates structure and order from the disorder. So what does this have to do with business practices?

Considering the laws of thermodynamics, in 1989, Robèrt drafted a paper describing the system conditions for sustainability. After soliciting others' opinions and achieving scientific consensus, his efforts became TNS's system conditions of sustainability and what is now called the framework for strategic sustainable development (FSSD).[9],[‡] The organization enabling this framework within cities and organizations is TNS Consultancy.

The framework's definition of sustainability includes system conditions that lead to a sustainable society.

In this sustainable society, nature should *not* be subject to systematically increasing:

---

‡See Broman and Robert (2017).

1. Concentrations of substances extracted from the Earth's crust.
2. Concentrations of substances produced as a by-product of society.
3. Degradation by physical means.

And in that society, people are not subject to systematic social obstacles[10] to the following:

1. Health
2. Influence
3. Competence
4. Impartiality
5. Meaning making

Positioned instead as the principles of sustainability, to become a sustainable society, economy, industry, supply chain, business, or individuals, we must:

1. Eliminate our contribution to the progressive buildup of substances extracted from the earth's crust (e.g., heavy metals and fossil fuels).
2. Eliminate our contribution to the progressive buildup of chemicals and compounds produced by society (e.g., dioxins, polychlorinated biphenyls (PCBs), dichlorodiphenyltrichloro-ethane (DDT), and other toxic substances).
3. Eliminate our contribution to the progressive physical degrada-tion and destruction of natural processes (e.g., overharvesting forests, paving over critical wildlife habitat, and contributions to climate change).
4. Eliminate exposing people to social conditions that systemati-cally undermine people's capacity to avoid injury and illness (e.g., unsafe working conditions, a nonlivable wage).
5. Eliminate exposing people to social conditions that systemat-ically hinder them from participating in shaping the social systems they are part of (e.g., suppression of free speech, or neglecting opinions).

6. Eliminate exposing people to social conditions that systematically hinder them from learning and developing competencies individually and together (e.g., obstacles to education, or personal development).

7. Eliminate exposing people to social conditions that systematically imply partial treatment (e.g., discrimination, or unfair selection to job positions).

8. Eliminate exposing people to social conditions that systematically hinder them from creating individual meaning and cocreating common meaning (e.g., suppression of cultural expression, or obstacles to cocreation of purposeful conditions).

A review of your organization's practices and infractions of these sustainability principles forms a baseline understanding that leaders and organizations can use to focus resources and efforts to bring about change. A five-level framework applied to planning and assessment can help any organization better determine why and how to approach

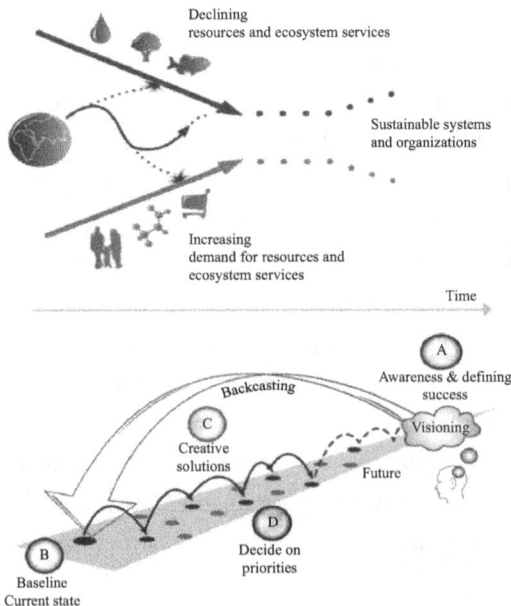

Figure 2.1 The FSSD funnel and ABCD application

change management initiatives. The five levels are the system, success, strategic, actions, and the use of tools.

At the **Systems level**, you need to understand the system in which you operate and the natural laws that define the biosphere and societies' relationship with the biosphere. **Success** is based on the sustainability principles and outlines the minimum requirements for success. The sustainability principles become the minimum and foundation for your operating manual. **Strategic** guidelines should guide decision making processes. Using an ABCD planning process, backcasting from your vision of the future provides guidelines for socially sustainable processes of relating transparency, cooperation, openness, inclusiveness, and involvement.[11] **Actions** come from prioritized steps put into action while following strategic guidelines for success in the systems. Finally, applying the appropriate **Tools** includes management techniques and monitoring processes to guide the implementation of strategic planning.

To illustrate the issue of sustainability, the FSSD uses the image of a funnel to demonstrate how decreasing resource availability and increasing consumer demand for those resources will eventually intersect, leading to a breakdown of the system (Figure 2.1). If, however, a company moves toward designing and operationalizing regenerative products, processes, and systems, resources and demand can continue forward on a sustainable path.

How can any firm or project team apply the FSSD? A simplified approach (much like Deming's Plan, Do, Check, Act) instead positions Awareness, Baseline, Create a Vision, and Down to Action to form the acronym ABCD, which describes the four steps of the framework to demonstrate its simplicity and power.

- *Awareness*: Work to create awareness of the idea of sustainability among stakeholders. Begin internally among managers, cross-functional teams, and within function champions, include line workers, purchasing, and drivers of trucks. When ready, (meaning when you can demonstrate capabilities and alignment with your value proposition). create awareness externally by releasing information first to your key customer(s) and suppliers and then release this information publicly.

- *Baseline*: Take a close look at all aspects of operations, from the stage-gate product design process, to management decision making and KPIs. Audit/benchmark current operations to understand the "as is" state and help determine the "to be" state and performance metrics. Include metrics such as CO_2 and GHG emissions, other forms of waste and social performance, transportation system design, supply chain practices, and employee and driver awareness.
- *Create a Vision*: Take what the baseline produced to see where you want to be in the future. Find opportunities for innovation. Set high goals. Define how you will measure success. From these goals, *backcast* to current operations and decision making utilizing systems thinking to see how decisions today will or will not move you closer to the future vision.
- *Down to Action*: Prioritize goals. Assess projects and initiatives by asking if they take your firm toward or away from its vision. Make the business case for return on investment; is this a good sustainable value added (SVA)? Create a contingency plan to anticipate risk management factors such as regulatory and cost-structure changes.

By following this framework, whole communities such as Whistler British Columbia, Madison Wisconsin, and Santa Monica California have strategically integrated sustainability into their planning. Multinational corporations such as Nike and IKEA (to name a few) have applied it to operations. The application of FSSD lends itself well to integrating supply chains and applied systems thinking to improve business model alignment of critical customers, capabilities, and value propositions. The result, a collective vision of the future, the use of tools including life cycle assessment (LCA), GHG protocol, environmental management systems (EMS), environmental and social metrics, and even integrated, closed-loop systems where waste is captured and turned into raw material inputs to turn the vision into a reality.

A brief case study highlights how strategic sustainable development can be applied to a firm, the integration opportunities for sustainability, and extensions to sustainable S^3CM.

Case Study: Applying the FSSD Within Aura Light

Compiled by Velika Talyarkhan[§]

Aura Light, a sustainable lighting company and Blekinge Institute of Technology (BTH) in Sweden, had a long-term consulting partnership that led to Aura Lighting changing its strategic direction. In 2009, Martin Malmos, Aura Light CEO, announced plans to make some major changes within the organization based on BTH's introduction to the FSSD and the support of a specialist sustainability consultancy, TNS.

Aura Light started out as a sustainable company from its inception in 1930 as LUMA. LUMA was founded as a reaction to the Phoebus cartel, comprising of Philipps GE, Osram, and others who were campaigning for the planned obsolescence of light bulbs. As it evolved, Aura Light's business model was to provide long-life fluorescent light sources to commercial clients and was looking to become "the most sustainable lighting company." Initially, Aura Light examined moving from fluorescent light solutions to LED solutions. The scarce metals and phosphates used in the LEDs could be recycled, but relying on consumers to recycle the products would not be efficient enough to avoid the sustainability impacts altogether. Aura Lighting decided to make even more extensive changes and shift its business model entirely from selling light products to selling light-as-a-service (LaaS). This would allow the company to control the materials at the end of use. In parallel, Aura Light would also conduct research on LEDs composed of alternative metals.[12]

[§]Velika Talyarkhan, Graduate Research Assistant, Duquesne University MBA+Sustainability program.

Defining Success

The first step was developing a shared vision of the future, creating a company with regenerative properties. It was crucial for the new vision to uphold the sustainability principles and avoid:

1. The systematic increase of concentrations of substances extracted from the Earth's crust
2. The systematic increase of concentrations of substances produced by society
3. The systematic physical degradation of nature and natural processes

The potential for people to be subject to structural obstacles to:

4. Health
5. Influence
6. Impartiality
7. Meaning-making[13]

TNS conducted a workshop with the Aura Light project team to set the scope of the assessment and conduct a preliminary baseline assessment. TNS conducted a sustainable life cycle assessment (SLCA) following the first workshop. TNS then facilitated a workshop with Aura Light managers four months later, which enabled the company to cocreate its new vision: "Aura Light's vision is to become the global leading partner for sustainable lighting solutions to professional customers." The definition of success is further described as follows in Table 2.1 as Aura Light's pillars for success and core values.

Redesigning the System With the ABCD Process[¶]

A—Vision

This stage was discussed previously in "defining success." The vision was agreed as "Aura Light's vision is to become the global leading partner for sustainable lighting solutions to professional customers."

[¶]The following section is summarized from França, César, Broman et al's paper.

Table 2.1 Aura Light's pillars of success

Pillars of success	Desired achievements
Innovation for tomorrow *We develop clean technology for a sustainable future*	• Designed for maximum energy efficiency • Designed for sustainable energy sources • Designed for recycling, closed-loop systems • No scarce metals or substances that risk increasing in concentration in nature • No health and safety risks • New ways of providing light
Smart solutions for users and society *We develop and supply sustainable lighting solutions for professional users*	• Challenge customers toward sustainability • One stop shop for lighting • Long life for resource efficiency • Energy efficiency • Safe working environment • Working recycling infrastructure, supply chains • Financial solutions to drive investments in clean technology
Our people and partners for change *We drive development toward a sustainable society*	• We attract, empower, and retain creative professionals • Our employees are empowered to lead the change • We share and develop competence in sustainability • We develop partnerships with customers, suppliers, communities, nongovernmental organizations, universities, and governments
Responsible business operations *We create sustainable operations throughout the value chain*	• Sustainable raw materials sourcing • Energy efficiency and sustainable energy sources • Optimized logistics and sustainable transports • Waste is avoided, reduced, or recycled • Only sustainable emissions • A healthy work/life balance and a safe workplace • A positive impact in the local communities

B—Assess the Current State

This stage was conducted in two steps:

Stage 1: Mapping the current business model using the FSSD-Business Model Canvas framework and LCA.

Stage 2: Mapping the current value network and analyzing its sustainability implications. A questionnaire was utilized to analyze the stakeholder relationships.

The outcome for step B was identifying the need to change the revenue stream to move from a product-selling business model to an LaaS business model. In its existing model, Aura Light's sole revenue stream was product sales. The challenges of moving to an LaaS business model included:

1. Providing confidence to investors about recovering goods if customers failed to pay fees.
2. Moving sales focus of physical products from a one-way flow of materials to reuse/recycling model.
3. Management routines and incentives are set up for selling (more of) physical products.
4. Addressing the potential skills gap within the design group and sales, whose competencies are adapted to designing and selling physical products.
5. Low levels of integration between the Aura Light design group and other functions such as business development, procurement, sales, and auditing.
6. The attention and communication around sustainability performance are mainly linked to energy-efficiency and not so much to the other sustainability aspects as informed by the FSSD sustainability principles.
7. Varying levels of sustainability competency and awareness in Aura Light's value network partners.
8. Clearly communicating the implications of the top-management's desired shift toward a more service-oriented business

model to all employees, value network partners and customers, who are only used to owning their light installations.

C—Brainstorming to Close the Gap

A second workshop was conducted to brainstorm actions and prioritize. Participants brainstormed and used a context-mapping tool to list possible solutions by theme. Workshop participants were encouraged to think creatively, with the only limitations being compliance with the FSSD's eight sustainability principles.

In addition, the participants considered three aspects of the life cycle (raw material, production, logistics and installation, use of end product, end of life) to prototype and prioritize actions:

- What had already been done?
- What Aura should stop doing?
- What Aura Light should start doing?

During the analysis, capacity building and cross-functional expertise became a key enabler for the implementation of a new business model.

The following table summarizes the themes that emerged during the session and some of the solutions proposed:

Theme	Solutions
Selling light as a service (LaaS)	• Create a new financial model, removing high installation cost for customers and incentivizing shift to new technology by removing lighting installation from customer's balance sheet. Establish a financing mechanism
	• Develop competence and capacity in the design group to work with the whole value network to develop LaaS offers (e.g., take-back offer structure)
	• Provide full maintenance and repair and reuse systems after upgrading
Sustainable Product-Service System (PSS)	• Multistakeholder cooperation to create more unique PSS offerings to differentiate and prevent copying

(Continued)

(Continued)

Theme	Solutions
	• Identify supply chain partners for capacity building • Align reporting and management approach to shift from a product to service-oriented company
Personalized energy houses and smart sustainable grids	• Develop capacity in business development and sales group to target appropriate decision makers in companies, widen value proposition to include sustainable cities • Value creation for "stranded" company assets (e.g., adding traffic monitoring function to street light pole)

D—Prioritization

In the final phase, Aura's CEO and decision makers selected a business model from the options developed in phase C. The most optimal models were prototyped, and the resulting LaaS model is as follows:

Aura's Progress

To date, several actions have been taken, including the establishment of Aura Finance, partnerships with luminaire companies, including the acquisition of Zobra and Noral, and further investments into the sustainability impacts of product development. From the capability development perspective, new employees are required to attend basic sustainability training, with further rollouts to be developed in the future.

The company's sustainability goals have also been mapped based on the new vision and progress made accordingly, as reported in their annual report.

Summary and Next Steps

Information within this chapter has looked at the risk of waiting to change, the trends in sustainability, systems integration opportunity, and a generalizable approach to understanding how your organization can assess, prioritize, and plan for strategically aligned sustainability initiatives. The Aura Light cast study shows how one organization has integrated

Table 2.2 Business canvas map (BCM) prototype of one new business model options for Aura light[14]

Key partners	Key activities	Value proposition LaaS	Customer relationships	Customer segments

• Aura Finance
• LED-Providers
• Cards-Providers
• Drivers-Providers
• Sensors-Providers
• Final Assemblers
• Education Partners
	• Contracts
	• Orders
	• Invoicing
	• Sales
	• Delivery
	• Maintenance
	
	Key Resources
	• Materials Technology
	• Employees
		Light as a Service	• Personal Assistance
			• Cocreation
			• Web-Enabled Services
			
			Channels
			• Subsidiaries
			• Sales Force
			• Distribution Chain
			• Trade Shows
				• Municipalities
				  ○ Industry
				  ○ Office
				• Retail

Cost Structure • Development Costs • Fixed Costs • Operation Costs			**Revenue Streams** • Monthly Payment for Light Service • Provided as Contracted	

Table 2.3 Aura Light sustainability goals[#]

Success factors	Focus goals	Results and operations
Innovations for the future	• Aura Light's product development process will ensure the production of sustainable solutions	• Continued focus on LED solutions and modularity • Sustainability factors implemented early in our product development projects
Smart lighting	• 90% of our sales come from Long Life products and solutions	• Results: 70% (target: 90%) • The reason why we have not achieved the objective is largely due to the change process that our operations are undergoing. For example, since the start value was set in 2010, sales of luminaries, has been implemented and grown substantially
	• 50% of our sales come from energy-saving products and solutions	• Results: 61% (target: 50%)
Employees and partners	• Our vision of sustainable lighting is communicated and understood by our customers	• We have been reporting in accordance with GRI since 2012 • Customer training and "lighting schools" with the focus mainly on LED, luminaires and sensors have been implemented in different countries
	• Our employees have the opportunity and the skills to integrate sustainability into their work	• All policies have been reviewed and approved by the Board of Directors • New working method for implementing sustainability factors at an early stage of product development projects

(Continued)

Table 2.3 (Continued)

Success factors	Focus goals	Results and operations
Responsible business operations	• Our emissions of carbon dioxide will decrease in relation to our sales	• From now on we also climate compensate for inbound freights
	• More than 95% of the waste from production will be recycled	• Results: 88%. Continued improvement in sorting and materials used in production, which are now recycled.
	• 40% of chemicals containing substances from the PRIO (health and safety risk management tool) list will be phased out	• Results: 42% has been phased out
	• The sustainability efforts of our main suppliers are evaluated and monitored through efficient processes	• Work with supplier audits is now an implemented process. Proposed measures from Aura Light were dealt with in a satisfactory way

Aura Light's Annual and Sustainability Report, www.auralight.com/fi/discover-us/sustainable-lighting/sustainability-report.

sustainability internally with the use of the FSSD and new options to engage their supply chain. Building on Chapter 1, we are attempting to take this complex paradigm of sustainability and breaking it down into constituent parts focusing on systems integration. In doing so, we are not trying to focus on the environmental and social problems of organizations. Instead, we want you to see the strategic sustainable development opportunities for what they are, systems level understanding that goes beyond manufacturing processes, the requirements for defining and measuring success, strategic guidelines, and actions supported by tools that will be expanded upon in the following chapters.

Applied Learning: Action Items (AIs)—Steps You Can Take to Apply the Learning From This Chapter

AI: What sustainability principles are most relevant to your organization?

AI: How would you define success when integrating sustainability into new initiatives?

AI: What sustainability trends are influencing your industry?

AI: Can you identify integrated systems within your organization or supply chain?

AI: What strategic guidelines for decision making are already in place, and how can sustainability be further integrated into these guidelines?

Further Readings

Broman, G. I. and K. H. Robért. "A Framework for Strategic Sustainable Development." *Journal of Cleaner Production* 140 (2017): 17–31.

Nidumolu, R., C. K. Prahalad, and M. R. Rangaswami. "Why Sustainability Is Now the Key Driver of Innovation." *Harvard Business Review* (2009): 65–64.

Sroufe, R., R. Atkins, and S. Curkovic. "Purchasing and Supply Management Empowerment in the New Product Development Process." *International Journal of Value Chain Management* 14, no. 4 (2023): 459–480.

United Nation's Sustainable Development Goals, for some context regarding what is happening in regards to environmental AND social opportunities for improving supply chains … https://sustainabledevelopment.un.org/sdgs.

Zimon, D., J. Tyan, and R. Sroufe. "Drivers of Sustainable Supply Chain Management: Practices to Alignment With UN SDGs." *International Journal for Quality Research* 14, no. 1 (2020).

PART 2

The Foundations of S³CM

CHAPTER 3

Sustainability—Generating a Strategic Competitive Advantage

Is There Demand for Sustainability?

Underlying the information within this chapter is a critical assumption—there is a demand for products and services that are sustainable. There is strong evidence indicating that customers (especially in economically developed markets and emerging markets) are, in fact, demanding products that are more sustainable. Consider the following statistics (McKinsey-NiesenIQ, 2023):[1]

- In a recent McKinsey U.S. consumer sentiment survey, more than 60 percent of the respondents indicated that they'd pay more for a product with sustainable packaging.
- A recent study by NielsenIQ found that 78 percent of U.S. consumers say that a sustainable lifestyle is important to them.
- Products making ESG claims averaged 28 percent cumulative growth over the past five-year period, versus 20 percent for products that had so claim.
- Consumers are shifting their spending toward products with ESG-related claims.
- Companies have a greater ESG impact and a better chance of achieving outsize growth if they incorporate high-impact ESG-related claims across multiple categories and products.

In other words, consumers and businesses are interested in sustainable products and services, and in the companies that produce them. Sustainability and sustainable supply chain management are about meeting and exceeding customer needs in new, more efficient, dynamic and effective ways.

Objectives

1. Understand how leading companies are taking advantage of the sustainability opportunity.
2. Recognize the role of business models in making sustainability a strategic imperative.
3. Appreciate the importance of increasing transparency in developing environmental and social sustainability capacity.

Paul Polman Transforms Unilever

Most people know Unilever, an Anglo-Dutch multinational consumer goods company. Its products include food, beverages, cleaning agents, and personal care products. It is the world's third-largest consumer goods company in terms of sales revenue (just after Procter & Gamble and Nestlé). One indication of Unilever's success and global reach is that over 200 million times a day someone in the world is using a Unilever product. Most CEOs would be happy to live with this status quo. Not Paul Polman.

His view is to transform Unilever from a company that does well financially to one that positively contributes to society and the environment. To undertake this transformation, Polman is shifting Unilever's focus. At the heart of this new focus is the Unilever Sustainable Living Plan.[2] The Living Plan identifies seven new key strategic supply chain imperatives, with the following goals:[3]

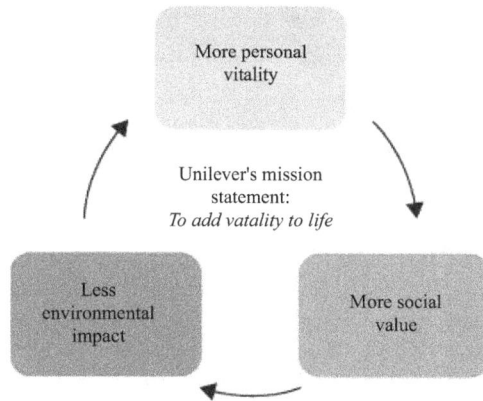

Unilever's approach to sustainability

The Key Seven Strategic Supply Chain Imperatives

- *Health and Hygiene*: Unilever will help more than a billion people to improve their hygiene habits and bring safe drinking water to over half a billion people.
- *Nutrition*: Unilever will double the proportion of the product portfolio that meets the highest nutritional standards, thus helping people achieve a healthier diet.
- *Greenhouse Gases*: It is Unilever's goal to halve the GHG impact of products across their life cycle (from sourcing to product use and disposal).
- *Water*: Unilever aims to halve the water usage associated with the consumer use of its products. The emphasis on this objective will be greatest in those countries that are populous and water scarce, countries where Unilever expects much of its future sales growth to take place.
- *Waste*: Unilever's goal is also to halve the waste associated with the disposal of its products.
- *Sustainable Sourcing*: Unilever's goal is to increase the amount of agricultural raw materials sourced sustainability from 10 to 30 percent by 2012, to 50 percent by 2015, and ultimately to 100 percent by 2020.

- *Better Livelihoods:* Unilever's goal is to link into the supply chain more than 500,000 smallholder farmers and small-scale distributors so that they can benefit by working with Unilever.

When we look at Paul Polman's vision of Unilever's future, we see a potentially risky vision. One that raises the question of whether a vision that so closely embraces sustainability (from an environmental and social perspective) can really be sustainable (as measured from a business perspective). Yet, it is a vision that Polman is now projecting onto Unilever as he looks to the developing countries to be the source, not only of future demand and population growth but also of future supply. This new vision is necessary to achieve this shift in strategic focus from the developed to developing countries.

That issue will be explored in this chapter, as we develop a deeper level of what sustainability is and is not and how sustainability can be a strategic weapon, rather than a legal constraint. This chapter is important because it is here that we establish many of the critical concepts on which an efficient and effective sustainable supply chain is built.

Understanding Sustainability

The triple bottom line (TBL) tries to address the sustainability opportunity by measuring it in accounting terms (i.e., dollars) so that management can identify those areas where it is doing a good job and areas where more work is required. First coined by Elkington (1994), this concept demands that the company be responsible not simply to stockholders but rather to the stakeholders. Stakeholders, in this case, refer to anyone who is affected either directly or indirectly by the firm's actions, including customers, workers, suppliers, investors, and even the environment. The goal of the TBL is to report and influence the firm as they affect financial, environmental, and social performance.

The TBL and the approach introduced in this book are not substitutes; rather, they are complements. The TBL identifies the goals to be achieved (measuring the financial, environmental, and social performance), but not how to achieve the balance or the best level of performance. The approach laid out in this chapter helps you better understand your options. It provides you with the foundations for successfully implementing and maintaining the TBL over time. In some ways, the TBL may understate the focus of sustainability. The TBL views the three dimensions as areas to be measured. Although important, this view may not focus attention on what these three areas truly are—investments into three forms of capital—economic, natural, and social. As assets, these areas should generate returns that can be measured and managed appropriately to ensure positive rates of return and an IBL.

Sustainability is, in general, a poorly understood concept because it has been interpreted in many different ways. According to diction- ary.com,[*] sustainability has two definitions:

1. The ability to be sustained, supported, upheld, or confirmed.
2. *Environmental Science.* The quality of not being harmful to the environment or depleting natural resources, and thereby supporting long-term ecological balance.

These two definitions highlight some of the reasons that confu- sion surrounds this concept. In the first definition, we can see the notion of *business sustainability*—developing an approach built around the business model that ensures that the value proposition (and the underlying business model) offered by the firm continues to be attractive to the key customers targeted by the firm and that this value proposition is supported by the appropriate set of capabilities. The second definition focuses on *environmental sustainability*. This is sustainability that deals with our ability to reduce the harm to the environment and to reduce the demands on natural resources (thus preserving them for tomorrow's generations). These definitions interestingly overlook the growing importance of *social sustainability*. This is sustainability that deals with an enterprises ability to compete in the marketplace while also reducing harm to employees and communi- ties in which the enterprise operates and engages in economic systems.

---

[*]http://dictionary.reference.com/browse/sustainability?s=t, last accessed May 22, 2024.

While each are different, the reality is that all types of sustainability are necessary if there is to be true business sustainability—long-term viability of both the business models and the resources and stakeholders needed to implement such business models. This realization offers a marked contrast to what we have seen in the past and what Freedman (1970) claims that "the social responsibility of business is to increase profits."

In the past, economic, environmental, and social sustainability were seen as presenting managers with a critical trade-off. That is, if you wanted to do well from a business perspective, you had to be willing to sacrifice environmental or social performance. Conversely, if you focused on improving environmental or social sustainability, you did so at the expense of profit. This perspective can be regarded as the "OR" approach—what do you want?—better profits or less pollution? We now know this is often a misleading trade-off.

Increasingly we are seeing business, environmental, and social sustainability as tightly interlinked. That is, by focusing on environmental sustainability, we preserve resources, minimize negative impacts on people, and ensure our continued ability to satisfy customer demands—both today and into the future. Not only these actions are not only

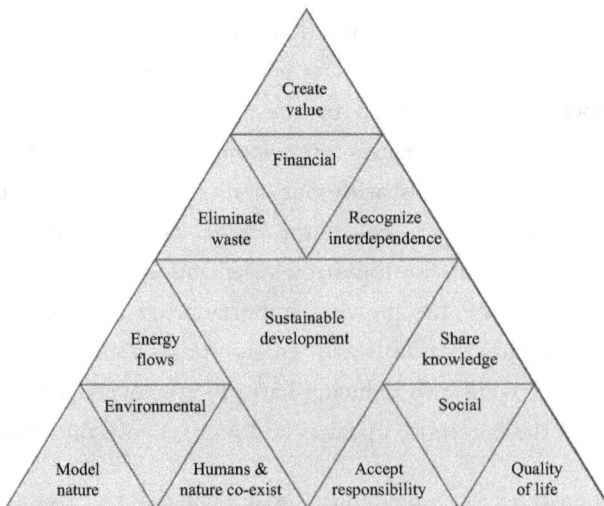

Figure 3.1 Sustainability and its business implications[4]

conducive to business sustainability, but they also help improve both top-line and bottom-line performances. Consequently, we can see the emergence of the "AND" approach—an approach where all forms of sustainability are simultaneously attainable. Yet, it is important to note that the presence of environmental or social sustainability by itself is not enough to ensure business sustainability. The authors of this book take the view that environmental and social sustainability facilitate business sustainability. It is also this view that drives a vision of sustainability portrayed in Figure 3.1.

Sustainability and Its Implications for the Firm

Sustainability is attractive because it can and does affect various aspects of corporate performance and competitive advantage:

- Natural resource, energy, and operational efficiency resulting in reduced input and overhead costs, fewer regulatory sanctions, reduced waste expenses, and enhancing the ability of the firm to conserve capital for implementing long-term growth strategies.
- Enhanced ability to attract and keep better quality employees, resulting in a better ability to retain experienced workers. This prevents the loss of corporate knowledge and expertise, reduced training costs, lowers employee absenteeism, increases worker productivity, and ultimately helps to attract and keep the best talent.
- Reduced risks from mitigating higher costs of energy, water, and waste, fewer exposures to supply chain disruptions, and reduced exposure to the risk of a price on GHG emissions.
- Better financial operations can help improve relationships with investors and also make the stock more attractive to potential investors. Other benefits include lower insurance premiums, decreased borrowing costs, and enhanced access to financial capital.
- Improved revenue streams, better marketing, and communication as sustainability offers the firm a way of expanding its

customer base by attracting those customers for whom sustainability is important. Such customers are often less price sensitive.
Furthermore, because these customers are often better educated
and earning more, they tend to buy more and more frequently.
Focusing on sustainability enables the firm to differentiate
its products, and to improve brand image and brand equity
(important corporate assets). For a growing number of firms,
financial and nonfinancial (sustainability) information is now
communicated into one integrated report.[5]

In other words, sustainability, if implemented properly, affects both
the top line (increased sales) and the bottom line (increased profit)
through the one-two punch of increased revenue and decreased costs.
This now moves the TBL into a new paradigm of IBL performance.[†]
However, for us to develop a better understanding of how these
concepts interact, we must first understand each concept in isolation—
beginning with environmental sustainability.

Environmental Sustainability

Environmental sustainability involves more than simply reducing
pollution; it is a broad-based approach that focuses on reducing
waste while improving performance across an IBL. The concern over
sustainability has influenced buying policies and sourcing requirements
found in Canada, the United States, the European Union, China,
and Australia. Companies such as Alcoa, Best Buy, Dell, Steelcase,
Phillips, Walmart, Coca-Cola, Ford, Toyota, Unilever, Disney Entertainment, and the InterContinental Hotels are now explicitly considering
sustainability in their planning at both the strategic and operational
levels. To appreciate the commitment that some companies have made
to environmental sustainability, consider the approach taken by Walt
Disney Resorts.

[†]See Sroufe (2018) for more information on the IBL.

Walt Disney is the world's largest media and entertainment company and is increasingly a leader in environmental sustainability. To achieve this status, Disney has taken the following steps:

1. *Cutting Emissions*: Walt Disney plans to cut carbon emissions by half, reduce electronic consumption by 10 percent, reduce fuel use, halve the garbage at its parks and resorts, and ultimately achieve net zero direct GHG emissions and landfill waste. Consequently, Walt Disney World has been designated as Florida Green Lodging Certified, and they use an internal price on carbon dioxide emissions when evaluating projects.[‡]

2. *Recycling and More*: The Disney Harvest Program, founded in 1998, distributes nearly 50,000 pounds of food to the Second Harvest Food Bank every month (taken from food that has been prepared but not served at Disney's various restaurants and convention centers). All used cooking oil at Walt Disney Resort is collected and recycled into bio fuel, as are other products that are used by local companies. Food scraps are recycled into compost that is used locally as fertilizer. The Walt Disney Healthy Cleaning Policy aims to minimize the environmental impact of its cleaning products. The majority of props, vases, and containers used by the Disney floral team for events are made from reusable glass and plastics. Finally, every day, 10 million gallons of wastewater is reclaimed and used in irrigation systems and other similar applications.

3. *Preserving Wildlife*: When building Walt Disney World Resort in Orlando, the company set aside more than one-third of the land for a wildlife conservation habitat. This habitat forms the basis for Disney's Animal Kingdom Theme Park, educates guests on the importance of conservation and preserving the future.

Ultimately, these and other steps are part of Walt Disney's long-term environmental strategy of:

[‡]Putting a Price on Carbon, Carbon Disclosure Project. https://www.cdp.net/en/research/global-reports/putting-a-price-on-carbon

Table 3.1 Global 100 list—Top 50 firms (all North American firms are noted in bold)[6]

Rank	Company	Country	Rank	Company	Country
1	**Schnitzer Steel Industries**	USA	27	Vitasoy International Holdings	China
2	Vestas Wind Systems A/S	Denmark	28	City Developments Ltd	Singapore
3	Brambles Ltd	Australia	29	Neste Oyj	Finland
4	Brookfield Renewable Partners, LP	Bermuda	30	**Ecolab Inc**	USA
5	**Autodesk, Inc.**	USA	31	Kering SA	France
6	**Evoqua Water Technologies Corp.**	USA	32	Beijing Enterprises Water Group Ltd	China
7	Stantec Inc.	Canada	33	ASNM International NV	Netherlands
8	Schneider Electric, Inc.	France	34	Starhub Ltd	Singapore
9	Siemens Gamesa Renewable Energy SA	Spain	35	**SunPower Corp**	USA
10	Taiwan High Speed Rail Corp	Taiwan	36	**Xerox Holdings Corp**	USA
11	Dassault Systemes SE	France	37	Telus Corp	UK
12	Xinyi Solar Holdings Ltd	China	38	Unilever PlC	UK
13	Orstead A/S	Denmark	39	**HP Inc**	USA
14	Sims Ltd	Australia	40	**VMware Inc**	USA
15	Banco deo Brasil SA	Brazil	41	SAP SE	Germany
16	Rockwool A/S	Denmark	42	BCE Inc	Canada

(Continued)

Table 3.1 *(Continued)*

Rank	Company	Country	Rank	Company	Country
17	Johnson Controls International PLC	Ireland	43	Coloplast A/S	Denmark
18	Chr Hansen Holdings A/S	Denmark	44	Koninklijke KPN NV	Netherlands
19	Kone Oyj	Finland	45	Cogeco Communications Inc	Canada
20	Cascades Inc	Canada	46	**First Solar Inc**	USA
21	Atlantica Sustainable Infrastructure PLC	UK	47	Puma SE	Germany
22	**McCormick & Company**	USA	48	**Cisco Systems Inc**	USA
23	Novozymes A/S	Denmark	49	Atea ASA	Norway
24	Iberdrola SA	Spain	50	Konica Minolta Inc	Japan
25	BT Grouip PLC	UK			
26	**Alphabet Inc**	USA			

1. Zero waste
2. Net zero direct GHG emissions from fuels
3. Reducing indirect GHG emissions from electricity consumption
4. Net positive impact on ecosystems
5. Minimizing water use
6. Minimizing product footprint
7. Informing, empowering, and activating positive action for the environment

One strong indication of the growth and spread of environmental sustainability can be found in Table 3.1, which lists the top sustainable corporations in the world. In reviewing the listing of firms, it is interesting to note that the best company, from a sustainability perspective, is Schnitzer Steel Industries. Furthermore, out of the 50 companies listed, 11 firms are American.

Environmental sustainability is important to existing companies wanting to maximize the efficient use of resources and future companies who will eventually need access to the same resources. The most widely used definition of sustainability was offered by the United Nations Brundtland Commission in its report. This report stated that sustainability is "the ability to meet the needs of the present without compromising the ability of future generations to meet their own needs." In other words, what we do today to satisfy current needs will affect the future. This is one reason that the "cradle-to-grave" approach is no longer adequate for environmental sustainability (see The Story of Stuff).[7] Only about 1 percent of all the materials mobilized to serve America are actually made into products and still in use six months after the sale.[8] This means that 99 percent end up in landfills within six months. With a cradle-to-grave approach, we focus on returning waste to the ground. The problem is that this waste is essentially useless—it cannot be used to fulfil the original demand. It must be replaced by new, virgin material. It also is a missed opportunity for reclaiming raw materials and closed-loop systems (also called C2C, and if done properly, cradle to cradle to cradle). We are coming to the realization that the earth's resources are finite. As we use more today, there is less for future generations. This realization is not new; it is just becoming more prevalent and a larger opportunity for entrepreneurs to better leverage a circular economy and closed-loop supply chain systems to find solutions to this issue.

Social Sustainability

The second element, social sustainability, focuses attention on people, specifically human rights, health and safety, and quality of life in communities. Think of all the stakeholder groups a typical business directly affects: customers, workers, suppliers, and investors. In addition, businesses can indirectly affect the larger community and society.

Each of these stakeholder groups has their own needs and priorities (see Table 3.2).

Table 3.2 Key stakeholders and their expectations

Customers	Workers
Good "value" for their money products that are safe	Fair labor practices and a "living wage" that affords a reasonable standard of living
Privacy and protection of personal information	Safe working and living environments (both for themselves and the community)
Honesty in marketing and sales communications	
Integrity in fulfilling contracts and obligations.	Equal opportunities for advancement
Quick response to questions	Support for social and economic developments (e.g., schools, arts, parks, and charities)
System transparency, traceability	
Suppliers	**Investors**
Working with like-minded firms (who share similar values)	Providing competitive returns on investments
Opportunities for supplier development and improvement (learning within the supply chain)	Having a robust business model so that investors can expect consistent returns over time
Opportunities to grow—shared success	Integrity in reporting operating and financial conditions
Consistent application of rewards and punishments	Reduction of unreasonable risks and uncertainties (due to poor practices on the part of the firm and its operations management system)
Receiving a "fair" payment for goods and services provided	

As the examples in Table 3.2 illustrate, managers and supply chain members need to consider the needs and demands of many stakeholders when making choices about sources, process designs, labor policies, and so on. Numerous social issues are continuously highlighted by the media, pointing out potential inequities, or even the oppressive conditions that businesses and their suppliers might create, either knowingly or unknowingly. For example, in recent years, the media have brought attention to the exploitation of workers and small businesses in developing countries. As a result, more and more operations managers are participating in established "fair trade" practices. It also affects how companies buy and sell products. Fair trade is an organized social movement that seeks to help producers in developing countries, thus making for better trading conditions and promoting sustainability. Through fair-trade efforts, farmers are paid a price for their products, increasing revenues. This allows them to invest in better equipment, better food for their families, and allows them to send their children to school (rather than keeping them working on the farm to support the family). Many of the farmers affected often grow commodity products such as coffee. Consider the experiences of Starbucks with fair trade:

Starbucks Corporation is an international coffee company and coffeehouse chain. It is currently the world's largest coffeehouse company. In 2000, the company introduced a line of fair-trade products. Since then, this practice has evolved into a corporate-wide system aimed at guaranteeing ethical sourcing. To this end, it has worked with Conservation International to develop the Coffee and C.A.F.E. practices for coffee-buying. This comprehensive set of guidelines focuses attention on four areas:

1. Product quality
2. Economic accountability
3. Social responsibility
4. Environmental leadership

Social responsibility measures are evaluated by third-party verification to ensure safe, fair, and humane working conditions and adequate living conditions—they cover minimum wage, child labor, and forced labor requirements.

Starbucks bought over 428 million pounds of coffee, of which 367 million pounds were from C.A.F.E.—practices-approved suppliers. The company paid an average price of $2.38 per pound, up from $1.56 per pound a year earlier. According to Conservation International, this premium has enabled farmers participating in C.A.F.E. practices to keep their children in school and to preserve the remaining forest on their land, while achieving higher crop performance. This program spans some 20 countries affecting over 1 million workers each year and impacts practices on 102,000 hectares each year (where a hectare is about 2.47 acres and in this case about 393 square miles a year). In terms of fair trade, Starbucks has paid an additional $16 million in fair-trade premiums to those producer organizations for social and economic investments at the community and organizational levels.[9,§] Fairtrade is but one social movement and differentiation strategy involving social responsibility.

If you think no one is keeping track of the social dimensions of your operations and those of your supply chains, you may be surprised to find your company on a list of poor-performing firms. Numerous organizations are measuring and ranking the operations and supply chain performance of publicly traded firms. These organizations include the well-known American business magazine *Forbes*, and established databases of socially responsible firms such as Kinder, Lydenberg, and Domini (KLD), that was taken over by Morgan Stanley Capital International (MSCI), and now Standard & Poor (S&P) Global provides access to this sustainability data on publicly traded firms. S&P Global's corporate sustainability assessment provides access to up to 1,000 ESG data points for individual companies assessed.[¶] You can now access ESG data through Bloomberg terminals. This is the same data used in socially responsible investing indices and be used to leverage other rankings by *Newsweek* purposefully looking at ESG performance.

[§]See their more recent Global Impact Report at https://stories.starbucks.com/uploads/2024/02/2023-Starbucks-Global-Impact-Report.pdf.

[¶]See S&P Global's ESG Data Intelligence at www.spglobal.com/esg/solutions/esg-data-intelligence for more details regarding this data.

Table 3.3 Forbes' most admired companies "best and worst in social responsibility"[10]

Most admired (2024)	Least admired[11]
1. REI	1. Exxon-Mobil
2. Subaru	2. Kraft/Heinz
3. H-E-B	3. Walmart
4. Sony	4. Chevron/Texaco
5. Samsung	5. GM
6. USAA	6. GE
7. Apple	7. Pfizer
8. Trader Joe's	8. Nestle
9. Jordan	9. Citi
10. Mary Kay Cosmetics	10. Dow

Among the leaders in this social dimension are firms such as REI, Subary, Sony, Samsung, Apple, and USAA (to name only a few). A listing of the most and least admired companies from a social responsibility perspective is in Table 3.3.

Deploying Social Sustainability

The social dimension of sustainability concerns the impacts an organization has on the social systems within which it operates, for example, reporting on human rights, local community impacts, diversity, and gender. The most comprehensive and widely accepted social sustainability reporting guidance is the Global Reporting Initiative's (GRI) guidelines. Within this framework, performance indicators are organized into categories: economic, environment, and social. The social category is broken down further by labor rights and decent work practices, human rights, society, and product responsibility subcategories. This measurement and reporting is done within the context of a materiality assessment and resulting matrix showing the level of stakeholder concern of sustainability issues in comparison to impacts on an organization.

Performance indicators are the qualitative or quantitative information regarding firm results or outcomes associated with the organization that is comparable and demonstrates change over time.** Disclosing firms will release information on their management approach, goals and performance, policies in place, who within the organization has responsibility for the performance indicators, training and awareness, and how the performance indicators are monitored. Examples of labor, human rights, society, and product responsibility from the GRI include the following:

Labor Practices are guided by several internationally recognized standards from the United Nations and the Convention on the Elimination of all Forms of Discrimination Against Women (CEDAW). For an understanding of these practices, reporting firms can draw upon two instruments directly addressing the social responsibilities of business enterprises: the International Labor Organization (ILO) Tripartite Declaration Concerning Multinational Enterprises and Social Policy, and the Organization for Economic Cooperation and Development (OECD) Guidelines for Multinational Enterprises. Practices include the composition of the workforce, full-time employees, benefits and retention rates, labor/management relations, occupational health and safety, employee training and education opportunities, diversity, equal opportunity, and equal remuneration for both women and men.

Human Rights practices take into account a growing global consensus that organizations have the responsibility to respect human rights. Human rights performance indicators require organizations to report on the extent to which processes have been implemented, on incidents of human rights violations, and on changes in the stakeholders' ability to enjoy and exercise their human rights during the reporting period. Among the human rights issues included are nondiscrimination, gender equality, freedom of association, collective bargaining, child labor, forced and compulsory labor, and indigenous rights.

Society practices focus attention on the impact organizations have on the local communities in which they operate, and disclosing how the risks that may arise from interactions with other social institutions are managed and mediated. In particular, information is sought on the risks

---

**Global Reporting Initiative at www.globalreporting.org/.

associated with bribery and corruption, undue influence in public policy making, and monopoly practices. Within social performance, community members have individual rights based on: Universal Declaration of Human Rights; International Covenant on Civil and Political Rights; International Covenant on Economic, Social, and Cultural Rights; and Declaration on the Right to Development.

Indicators of **product responsibility** address the aspects of a reporting organization's products and services that directly affect customers, namely, health and safety, information and labeling, marketing, and privacy. These aspects are primarily covered through disclosure on internal procedures and the extent to which there is noncompliance with these procedures. Reporting firms have the opportunity to provide disclosure on their management approach to customer health and safety, product and service labeling, marketing communications, customer privacy, and compliance.

This summary of social sustainability can be new and uncharted territory for many. For some well-known firms highlighted in this book, the social performance dimension is one more way to build brand. Social sustainability is still an emerging area for many to differentiate products, measure and manage typically overlooked aspects of value creation, and become an employer of choice while simultaneously building top-line *and* bottom-line growth.

Trends in corporate transparency and reporting are such that reporting financial performance is only a starting point. Over a decade ago, KPMG and others have demonstrated the start of integrated reporting of business, environmental, and social sustainability performance into one report.[12],[††] As we will see in this and the next chapter, the public disclosure of these performance metrics reveals a shift in corporate reporting, emerging views of sustainability, and an opportunity to leverage lean operations to realize the value created by sustainability.

[††] Also see the book "One Report" by Eccles and Krzus.

Transparency

Transparency is most notable through the broad expansion of corporate reporting. Gone are the days of producing and auditing only a financial report. Sustainability reporting is the practice of measuring, disclosing, and being accountable to internal and external stakeholders for organizational performance toward the goal of sustainable development. "Sustainability reporting" is a broad term considered synonymous with others used to describe reporting on economic, environmental, AND social impacts (e.g., an IBL, corporate responsibility reporting).[‡‡] A sustainability report should provide a balanced and reasonable representation of the sustainability performance of a reporting organization—including both positive and negative contributions. Sustainability reports based on international frameworks disclose outcomes and results that occurred within the reporting period in the context of the organization's commitments, strategy, and management approach. Reports can be used for, but not limited to, the following purposes:

- Benchmarking and assessing sustainability performance with respect to laws, norms, codes, performance standards, and voluntary initiatives.
- Demonstrating how the organization influences and is influenced by expectations about sustainable development.
- Comparing performance within an organization and between different organizations over time.

The urgency and magnitude of the risks to our collective sustainability cannot be understated. New measurement and reporting opportunities will make transparency about economic, environmental, *and* social impacts a fundamental component in effective stakeholder relations, investment decisions, and other market relations.[§§] Increasingly, it is difficult to find an annual report that omits any discussion of the sustainability activities of the firm. Yet, we must recognize that not all firms claiming to be sustainable are operating at the same level of

---

[‡‡]GRI.
[§§]Ibid.

Table 3.4 View of sustainability relationships

View of sustainability	Relationship (financial, environmental, and social sustainability)
Public relationships	Trade-off; you can be one or the other; focus on one dimension; environmental or social sustainability is a constraint
Waste management	Mixed—some trade-offs; more complementary
Value maximization	Simultaneity; integration; you have multiple types of sustainability; environmental and/or social sustainability is an opportunity and a strategic weapon

intensity. We argue that firms operate at one of the three levels of sustainability:

- Sustainability as public relations
- Sustainability as waste management
- Sustainability as value maximization

As we move from the first to the last, we see a broader application of sustainability (Table 3.4). We also see a different view of the dynamic relationships between environmental, social, and business sustainability.

However, each level must be explored separately to be understood.

Sustainability as Public Relations

Firms focusing on sustainability at this level are not really committed to all three dimensions. Management ultimately believes that there is a trade-off between profit and social or environmental sustainability— to do better on one dimension, you must do worse on another. They feel that they have been forced by external pressures (e.g., consumers, government, stockholders) to show that their firms are undertaking some form of environmental program.

Such programs, when implemented, are often copied from other firms. When implemented, there is little or no modification or customization of the programs and their associated practices.

Customization is important to ensure that newly adopted practices first fit the firm's unique corporate setting. Environmental programs also have to be extended and transformed in ways that create new value for the key customers. These programs are there so that management can point to their presence as proof of the firm's commitment to some level of sustainability.

Sustainability as public relations is all about "show"; if you are able to dig deeper, there is little of substance behind the show. When reporting, the firm looks for whatever evidence it can find that shows the firm is securing the benefits of sustainability. When implemented, the programs tend to be superficial—focusing on the symptoms rather than the root cause of pollution. Recycling is emphasized and reported rather than pollution prevention. Investments are made in initiatives, but little real progress is secured because management and corporate commitment to environmental sustainability is lacking. Sustainability as public relations sometimes manifests as "greenwashing" when stakeholders call out an organization for not truly being green.

Internally, sustainability is treated as a constraint—something that must be satisfied before the firm can turn its attention to what really is important. The programs and initiatives, when added, are often add-ons—present but poorly integrated. These programs are separate from the rest of the firm. Responsibility for environmental sustainability is not a total corporate responsibility (everyone is responsible) but rather something that is assigned to one department and few who are accountable for the programs. Performance is measured from the perspective of punishment avoidance or punishment incurred (e.g., number of fines, size of fines).

Finally, these firms are the first to drop or scale back initiatives in sustainability should the economy deteriorate (thus requiring firms to focus on cost savings) or should management feel that the external forces driving the emphasis on sustainability are diminishing. You may already know of some firms at this level of sustainability. We provide examples of more progressive firms in the next chapter as we continue exploring levels of sustainability with a focus on waste management, and value maximization in the next chapter.

Summary

This is a book about developing and maintaining a sustainable supply chain. Given the growing importance of sustainability, the goal of this chapter has been to develop a thorough and well-grounded understanding of this business paradigm. In this chapter, the following points were made:

- We need a more dynamic understanding of sustainability.
- Sustainability implementation and achievement affect the extent to which environmental and social performances are viewed as complementary or trade-offs.
- Supply chains and organizations are becoming more transparent.
- Sustainability can help with public relations, yet needs to be a strategic part of differentiation and competitive advantage.

With Chapters 1 and 2 as a foundation, we are now able to move toward the challenge of developing a sustainable supply chain. As we do so, there are more foundational elements to introduce—enhancing value, along with business model integration. That is the focus of the coming chapter.

Applied Learning: Action Items (AIs)—Steps You Can Take to Apply the Learning From This Chapter

AI: What companies in your own industry do you consider leaders in sustainability? Why?

AI: Search the web for social sustainability issues in your industry, does your organization have these same issues?

AI: Who is the most transparent company in your industry?

AI: Who are your organization's key stakeholders? Why?

AI: Conduct a self-audit of your firm's environmental and social sustainability practices.

AI: What public relations information has been issued by your firm that involves environmental or social performance?

AI: Where can you see IBL opportunities for value creation within your enterprise and supply chain?

Further Readings

Eccles, R. G. and M. P. Krzus. *The Integrated Reporting Movement: Meaning, Momentum, Motives, and Materiality.* Hoboken, NJ: John Wiley & Sons, 2014.

Epstein, M. J. and A. R. Buhovac, *Making Sustainability Work: Best Practices in Managing and Measuring Corporate Social, Environmental, and Economic Impacts.* Berrett-Koehler Publishers, 2014.

Hawkin, P. *Drawdown—The Most Comprehensive Plan Ever to Reverse Global Warming.* Penguin Books, 2017.

McDonough & Braungart. *Upcycle.* North Point Press, 2013.

S&P Global ESG Scores: www.spglobal.com/marketintelligence/en/solutions/sustainability-capital-iq-pro-platform#:~:text=Environmental%2C%20Social%20and%20Governance%20Raw%20Data%20Access,we%20assess%20in%20the%20S&P%20Global%20CSA.

CHAPTER 4

Sustainability—Reducing Waste, Enhancing Value

There is a simple rule about the environment. If there is waste or pollution, someone along the line pays for it.
—Lee Scott, Chief Executive, Walmart

Ask yourself a question—do you want to source materials or products from poorly performing companies? If the answer is *yes*, then go ahead and continue paying for excessive waste that is now measured in GHG emissions or poor social impacts in the form of labor practices. If the answer is no, then look for companies in your supply chain that are leveraging sustainability to enhance existing business models, differentiate products and services, and reduce or eliminate waste from processes.

- Lawrence Livermore National Laboratory estimates that in the United States, we waste more than 60 percent of our energy consumption. Electricity generation and transportation are the two largest contributors to this wasted energy.
- Walmart and Puma have found that over 92 percent of their GHG emissions come from their supply chains.
- Combustion engines used for transportation (i.e., your car) only convert 5 percent of energy to movement of the passenger, and only 20 percent of the power generated by burning gasoline reaches the wheels. The rest is lost in heat and friction and can cost upward of 20 cents per mile while we each drive over 14,000 miles on average in the United States.
  - Think about driving for 60 years, 14,000 miles a year with a vehicle averaging 25 mgp, and price for gas near $4 a gallon. You would be spending $134,400 for a lifetime of

movement, and wasting 80 percent of that, or over $100,000 with it going to heat and friction, not movement in an internal combustion engine.

- Electric vehicles are 90 percent efficient in converting energy to movement. One of the authors of this book generates electricity from solar Photovoltaic (PV) systems. With this approach to energy generation and use, it costs about one cent per mile to drive an electric vehicle, which is less than $9,000 for a lifetime of driving.

We should not willingly reward wasteful companies. S³CM is about realizing the full value from supply chains and operations.

Objectives

1. Understand the notion of waste as it provides new insight to sustainability.
2. Recognize the role of business models in making sustainability a strategic imperative.
3. Appreciate the importance of "Sustainable Value Added" for assessing sustainability.

Sustainability as Waste Management

Building on the three levels of sustainability introduced in Chapter 3, we now look at waste management. This approach to sustainability traces its roots to a simple but powerful observation made in Chapter 1—waste is simply anything that does not add value to a product or service. Waste has been the focus of lean systems (otherwise known as the Toyota Production System (TPS) or just-in-time (JIT) manufacturing). Lean systems, since they were first introduced into North America in the early 1980s, have developed a long track record of being highly successful when applied correctly.

In part, the successful spread of lean can be attributed to a three-year study on the impact of lean systems within the automotive industry. This study, conducted by Womack, Jones, and Roos (1990)[1] ended the debate about whether lean systems created real, lasting benefits.

Table 4.1 Performance characteristics for lean systems in various geographies

	Japanese in Japan	Japanese in North America	Americans in North America	All Europe
Performance				
Productivity (hrs/vehicle)	16.8	21.2	25.1	36.2
Quality (assembly defects/100 vehicle)	60	65.0	82.3	97.0
Layout				
Space (sq. ft/vehicle/yr)	5.7	9.1	7.8	7.8
Size of repair areas (as percentage of assembly space)	4.1	4.9	12.9	14.4
Inventories (days for eight sample parts)	0.2	1.6	2.9	2.0
Work force				
Percentage of workforce in teams	69.3	71.3	17.3	0.6
Job rotation (0 = none; 4 = freq)	3.0	2.7	0.9	1.9
Suggestions/employee	61.6	1.4	0.4	0.4
Number of job classes	11.9	8.7	67.1	14.8
Training of new production workers (hours)	380.3	370.0	46.4	173.3
Absenteeism	5.0	4.8	11.7	12.1
Automation				
Welding (percentage of direct steps)	86.2	85.0	76.2	76.6
Painting (percentage of direct steps)	54.6	40.7	33.6	38.2
Assembly (percentage of direct steps)	1.7	1.1	1.2	3.1

Source: Womack, J.P., D.T. Jones and D. Roos, *The Machine That Changed the World*, 92.

As shown in Table 4.1, the results showed that in the 1980s Japanese-owned automotive plants following lean were as much as 30 percent more productive than U.S.-owned plants using traditional methods—quite a turnaround from the situation in the 1930s. Furthermore, the

Japanese plants delivered cars with fewer defects, lower space requirements, and lower inventories. The data also showed that the Japanese
lean effect was significant whether the plant was located in Japan or in
the United States.

By treating pollution as waste, firms pursuing environmental
sustainability could leverage and build on their experiences with lean
to simultaneously achieve improved environmental performance. They
could draw on and use similar frameworks; they could also use many
of the same tools. The result—a low cost and, in many cases, a proven
way of reducing waste. To understand this approach, it is important that
we start with the foundations on which it is built—pollution and GHG
emissions as waste.

Pollution as Waste

One of the major objectives of any lean system is to reduce waste. Waste
can be identified as any activity that creates cost without contributing
an equal or greater level of value. This thinking is not new and can be
traced back to the work of Henry Ford in the early 1910s and 1920s.
Waste consumes but does not reward.

Something to think about: Of the approximately 100 quads of
energy used in the United States, over 67 percent is lost or rejected
energy; the two largest contributors to this waste include 36 percent of
this loss from electricity generation systems and 32 percent from the
transportation industry with these industries heavily reliant on fossil
fuels.[2] Further, the International Monetary Fund (IMF) finds that global
fossil fuel subsidies are over \$11M every minute. How much waste is
within your system, and who is paying for it?

Under the lean perspective, waste is a *symptom*. That is, it is the
result of problems elsewhere. It is also the result of problems within
processes (the fundamental unit of analysis for lean). Wastes of all
kinds, including GHG emissions, can be grouped into one of the seven
categories (Table 4.2). To these seven, many managers now add an
eighth category—waste of skills—not drawing on or using our people

Table 4.2 Seven types of waste

Waste	Symptoms	Root causes
Overproduction (processing more units than are needed)	• Extra inventory • Excessive floor space utilized • Unbalanced material flow • Complex information management • Disposal charges • Extra waste handling and treatment • High material, utility, waste costs • GHG emissions	• Product complexity • Misuse of automation • Long process setups • Unlevel scheduling • Overengineered equipment/capability • Lack closed-loop systems, reuse, and recycling • Poor market forecast • Extra inventory as a demand buffer
Waiting (resources wasted waiting for work)	• Underutilization of resources • Reduced productivity • Increase in investment • Idle equipment • Large waiting/storage rooms • Equipment running, not producing • Unnecessary testing	• Unbalanced work load • Unplanned maintenance • Long process setup times • Misuse of automation • Unlevel scheduling • Ineffective layout • Too much specialization
Transportation (units being unnecessarily moved)	• Extra handling equipment • Large storage areas • Over staffing • Damaged product • Extra paperwork and hand offs • Excessive energy consumption • Expedited shipments • GHG emissions	• Mislocated materials • Unlevel scheduling • Unfavorable facility layout • Poor organization/house-keeping • Unbalanced processes • Facility location, off-shoring • Quantity discounts

(Continued)

Table 4.2 (*Continued*)

Waste	Symptoms	Root causes
Processing (excessive or unnecessary operations)	• Extra equipment • Longer lead time • Reduced productivity • Extra material movement • Sorting, testing, inspection • Inappropriate use of resources • Excess energy consumption, waste, GHG emissions • Processing by products	• Product changes without process changes • Just-in-case logic • Lack of communication • Redundant approvals and inspections • Undefined customer requirements • Stop gap measures that become routine • Lack closed-loop systems, reuse, and recycling
Inventory (units waiting to be processed or delivered)	• Complex tracking systems • Extra storage and handling • Extra rework/hidden problems • Paperwork/documents • Stagnated information flow • High disposal costs • In-process packaging	• Just-in-case logic • Incapable processes (poor quality) • Unbalanced workload • Unreliable supplier shipments • Inadequate measurement and reward system • Future costs of commodities
Motion (unnecessary or excessive resource activity)	• Reduced productivity • Large reach/walk distances • Excess handling • Reduced quality • People/machines waiting	• Poor ergonomics/layout • Machine/process design • Nonstandardized work methods • Poor organization/housekeeping
Product defects (waste due to unnecessary scrap, rework, or correction)	• Rework, repairs, and scrap • Customer returns • Loss of customer confidence • Missed shipments/deliveries	• Lack of process control and error proofing • Deficient planned maintenance • Poor product design • Customer needs not understood

(*Continued*)

Table 4.2 (Continued)

Waste	Symptoms	Root causes
	• Hazardous waste generation • High disposal costs • GHG emissions	• Improper handling • Inadequate training

who understand the issues and opportunities more sustainable business practices provide to the best of their ability.

The Lean Approach

To reduce waste, we must study the processes, uncover the critical root causes, and then attack (and hopefully, eliminate) them with a goal of zero waste. We can draw on and use the following lean tools for attacking waste:

- Total productive maintenance (TPM): The processes and systems that work to identify and prevent all possible equipment breakdown through a combination of preventive maintenance by the employees, rigorous equipment design, and regular inspection of the equipment.
- Setup reduction: The processes used to reduce setup and changeover times with the goal of making output in smaller batches efficient.
- Statistical process control: The use of various statistical tools for analyzing the capabilities of a given process, and for monitoring its performance with the goal of flagging potential problems before they occur.
- Quality at the source (Q@S): The practice of eliminating defects at their origination points.
- Kaizen events: A short-term project (usually one to four days) aimed at improving an existing process. In that time period,

cross-functional team members document a process, assess different options for performance, and develop and document the implemented process changes.

- Process analysis/value stream mapping: Graphic mapping techniques that help managers understand the material and information flows as a product and how it makes its way through the process.
- Poka-yoke: Also known as fool-proofing. An emphasis on redesigning processes in such a way as to make mistakes either impossible or immediately apparent to the people involved.
- Standardization/simplification: A program whereby nonvalue-adding steps in a process are eliminated (simplification) and each step in the process is carried out in exactly the same way by every employee (standardization) so that waste can be identified and eliminated.

With the lean approach, the emphasis shifts from the outputs (i.e., pollution) to prevention (by focusing on the processes generating these wastes). Because we know that waste, such as pollution and GHG emissions, is the result of problems in one or more processes, to eliminate waste we have to focus on changing the appropriate processes. We will discuss these and other tools in more detail in this chapter.

This approach is highly attractive because its causal logic is straight-forward, the lead time for results is often fairly short (days, weeks, months), there is a strong and direct linkage between cause and effect, and there are significant opportunities for improvement. As discussed in Chapter 1, the following relationships are important to revisit.

- In ordinary firms, for every one unit of value added (defined either from a time or cost perspective), the processes typically adds 1,000 to 2,000 units of nonvalue.
- In world-class firms, for every one unit of value added, the processes typically adds 200 to 300 units of nonvalue.

In other words, there is a lot of opportunity for improvement, waste reduction, and interrelated benefits.

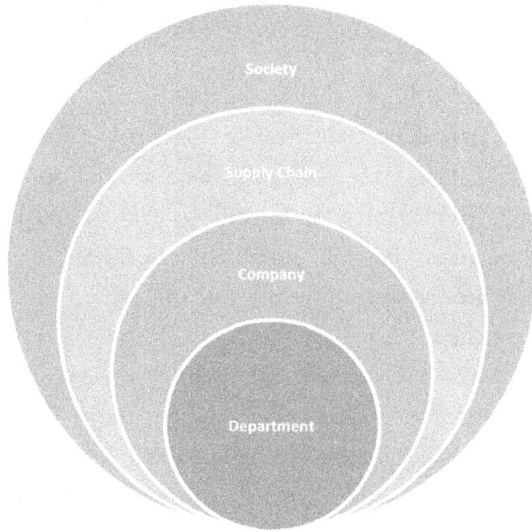

Figure 4.1 Scope of costs/benefits

Limitations of Sustainability as Waste Management

Despite its allure, the sustainability approach to waste management is not without its limitations. Two major drawbacks are particularly noteworthy, namely limitations of scope and focus. Understanding these limitations is crucial for a comprehensive evaluation of the approach.

Scope: Scope refers to the extent to which the costs/benefits are applied. When dealing with lean systems, we can measure costs and benefits at several levels (see Figure 4.1). First, we can measure it in terms of its impact on the department's performance. Of all the levels of analysis, this is the simplest and most direct to determine. Here, we are not interested in whether our actions affect those of the other departments. *The goal is to improve our level of performance.* Local optimization (at the expense of overall improvement) is accepted and prized. We can increase the scope to include the entire company, management leadership, and operations. Now, analysis and evaluation are more complex. We have to consider the impact of our actions on the integrated performance of other departments in the company, now we are getting at tactics. Similarly, we can increase the scope to include the supply chain and the community/society with longer-term, strategic implications.

As we increase the scope, analysis becomes more complex. However, as we increase the scope, we increase the opportunity to measure, manage, and affect more stakeholders. These are the opportunities for leadership, the CEO, chief financial officer (CFO), and in a growing number of companies, the chief sustainability officer (CSO). This new breed of leaders are "spearheading the true integration of material ESG issues into corporate strategy."[3]

When applied, lean systems tend to limit their scope to the first two levels—to the departments and to the company. For example, we can introduce a delivery system that emphasizes "milk runs" from our suppliers. Every day, we send a truck out to pick up supplies from our vendors. The truck goes out empty in the morning, but returns full at night. In it, we have enough components for the next day's production. From a typical "lean" perspective, this is good: inventory is low; we have enough inventory to keep production going. Yet, the problem with this approach is that by running our trucks in this manner, we are creating environmental waste in the form of increased energy consumption for the trucks (along with the associated waste and GHG levels). These impacts are typically felt, but not captured at the community level—a level beyond most organizations' focus.

Focus: In many lean systems, the impact of lean is measured in terms of cost savings or cost avoidance. These are two of the three levels in the performance pyramid (Figure 4.2). At the lowest level, the base, we have cost savings. With cost savings, we address existing problems in current products and processes. For example, we have an inefficient process. We apply the lean tools and eliminate the sources of waste, reduce the number of steps in the process, and lower the level of waste generated by the process. We can evaluate the impact of these changes by comparing the performance of the new, revised process with the level observed for the old process.

Cost avoidance is a higher level of performance. Here, we are not correcting past problems; we are avoiding them. This is a more powerful position, but one that is more difficult to assess. How do you measure

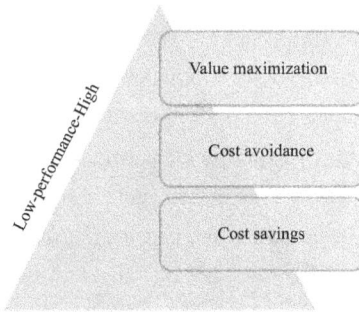

Figure 4.2 Performance pyramid

avoidance? As a sign at a well-known automotive user of lean puts it, "$P > S$" (Prevention is greater than Savings).

Yet, there is a third and higher level—value maximization. To achieve this level of performance, an approach different from the ones used for the prior two must be implemented. We can achieve cost savings and cost avoidance without ever considering issues as to who is the key customer, or what is the business model driving our firm. However, to increase revenue, we have to understand these and other issues from a larger systems perspective. To increase revenue (especially over time), we have to deal with issues such as value. When dealing with value and the firm's business model, we have changed the focus of sustainability from tactical to strategic. This is a critical transition and the third level of sustainability as value maximization is one in which environmental, social, AND business sustainability are simultaneously attainable.

Sustainability as Value Maximization

Of the three levels in the performance pyramid, value maximization is the most complex. Before we discuss what this level entails, we must first establish the foundations of this approach. At the heart of this approach are three critical concepts: (a) value, (b) business models, and (c) sustainable value maximization (this concept is defined in greater detail later on in this chapter).

Value

Value or the customer's assessment of the relative benefits and costs obtained by the acquisition of a specific good or service is becoming increasingly important in today's economy. While value begins with the customer, this concept is starting to have a significant impact of supply chains. As noted in a *Sloan Management Review* article by Melnyk, Davis, Spekman, and Sandor (2010),[4] there is a sea change taking place in supply chain management and at the heart of this change is value. In the past, supply chains were price driven (focused on cost savings) and strategically decoupled (not linked to how the firm competed in the marketplace). Now, they are increasingly becoming value driven and strategically coupled (linked to strategy).

It is important to recognize that value is customer specific. It is also important to recognize that not all elements of value are equally important. When a customer looks at the elements of value, how they respond and what they expect is driven by the type of traits they are dealing with. In general, these traits, which are often product-specific, can be classified into one of three categories:[5]

- Order Winners: These traits cause customers to choose a product or supply chain service over a competitor's offering, for example, better performance, lower price, environmental and social performance certification such as the Forest Stewardship Council, or fair trade. These are traits on which operations and the supply chain management system must excel and be transparent.
- Order Qualifiers: These are product or supply chain traits such as availability, price, or conformance quality that must meet a certain level for the product to even be considered by customers. The firm must perform acceptably on these traits (i.e., the products must meet certain threshold values of performance), usually at least, as well as competitors' offerings. In many cases, the customer may not be aware of any level of performance in excess of those minimum levels that they have established.

- Order Losers: Poor performance on these traits can cause the loss of either current or future business, for example, customers who shop at Target instead of Walmart due to labor practices.

In reviewing these categories, there are several factors to remember. First, order winners and order qualifiers form the basis for customers' expectations. Order losers, in contrast, result from customers' actual experiences with the firm and its operations management processes. They represent the gap between what the firm delivers and what customers expect. Second, order winners, order qualifiers, and order losers vary by customer. An order winner to one customer may be an order qualifier to another. Third, these traits vary over time. An order winner at one time may become an order qualifier at another point in time. Being able to identify and act on order winners offers the firm a critical strategic advantage.

While important by itself, the value concept becomes especially critical when implemented within a business model.

Business Models

The business model (as illustrated in Figure 4.3) can be viewed as the firm's method for doing business. It is the framework used by the firm for creating and maintaining dynamic environmental, economic, and social forms of value. Business models have also come to be recognized as a form of *intellectual property*—an asset that can be protected through a patent.

There are numerous examples of business models. For example, there is the "razor and blades" business model first developed by Gillette— give away the razor but make your money on the blades. There is also the "direct sales" business model so successfully used by Dell—sell computers directly to the end consumer with Tesla now using this same approach. As a final example, there is the "loyalty" business model. This model has been widely implemented in the airline industry (through the frequent flier program) and in the retail trade (e.g., as in Best Buy's Reward Zone program). With this model, consumers are rewarded for continuing to deal with the firm.

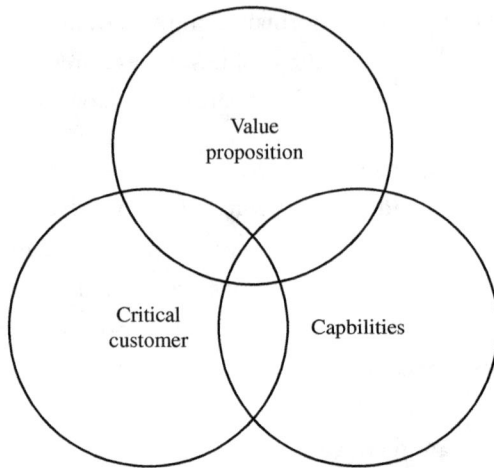

Figure 4.3 The foundations of the business model

Business models are part of business strategy, innovation, and sustainability.[6] The business model, by its very nature, is highly integrative in that it brings together into a meaningful whole the three elements—the key customer, the value proposition, and capabilities. To this point, this book has focused primarily on the capabilities element. Capabilities, while important, are not enough by themselves. As capabilities change over (due to factors such as technological innovation, capital investments, and process improvements), these changes have to be evaluated in terms of how they affect the other two dimensions. Furthermore, if the firm targets sustainability initiatives as a way to attract a new key customer, it must reevaluate the appropriateness of the current value proposition and capabilities (and make any necessary changes).

Increasingly, managers are talking about the need for better business models for three important reasons. First, there is strong empirical evidence that demonstrates the impact of business models of corporate performance. *Business Week* published a study, which showed that a firm with an innovative business model consistently outperformed competitors with innovative products, processes, and customer experiences (see Figure 4.4).[7]

Second, business models are inherently dynamic. They are intended to help two important groups of firms. For existing firms, it

Innovation type	Aver. stock return 2004 – 2007	Aver. revenue growth 2004 – 2007
Process	1.40%	1.60%
Product	3.10%	2.10%
Customer experience	2.50%	5.10%
Business model	16.60%	7.20%

Figure 4.4 Assessing the relative impact of an innovative business model

is recognized that they have to develop new and innovative business models to compete against growing competition. For new firms trying to get into an existing market, business models are important because they identify unique niches in the marketplace.

Third, business models are attracting attention because they provide a vehicle for converting new technology and innovations into economic value.[8] Innovation and new technology, in turn, are important because of the potential they offer the firm and the way in which they enable sustainability practices:[9]

- To serve new or existing customer segments whose needs have been neglected by existing competitors and their offerings.
- To serve new or existing customer segments whose needs are being poorly met by existing competitors and their offerings.
- To provide new ways of producing, delivering, or distributing existing (or new) products to existing (or new) customer segments.

Components of the Business Model

As we can see from Figure 4.3, the business model consists of three elements. It is important to understand what each element is and why it is important.

Key Customer(s): The starting and ending point for any effective and efficient supply chain operations is the customer. A *customer* is a person or organization who consumes the products of a process. A customer is not necessarily the end user; it could be the store manager or the purchasing agent. Almost all firms deal with multiple customers having varied desires and needs that change over time. This creates the dual challenge of keeping track of changing needs and identifying which customers' needs should be addressed and which should be ignored. Each firm has to identify its *key customers*.

The key customer is that group or segment that the firm has identified as being important. As Hal Mather, a manufacturing consultant, once said: the key customer is that customer segment that the firm "will profitably delight." When there is a conflict in meeting customer needs, it is always resolved in favor of the key customer.

Customers can be deemed key for a number of reasons. For example, a key customer may be responsible for largest amount of current or future sales of the firm, or it may be the one with the highest prestige. In the automotive industry, Toyota is often such a customer because of its very high quality and performance standards; a supplier working with Toyota is often viewed as a top-rate supplier.

Value Proposition: To attract these key customers, the firm must formulate and implement a *value proposition*, or a statement of what the firm offers the customer that is viewed attractive to the customer and is different from what is offered by its competitors. The value proposition is critical because it not only defines how the firm competes but also determines and shapes the types of products that the firm will (and will not) offer.

A well-designed value proposition possesses four traits: (a) it offers a combination of features that customers find attractive and are willing to pay for; (b) it differentiates the firm from its competitors in a way that is difficult to imitate; (c) it satisfies the financial and strategic objectives of the firm; and (d) it can be reliably delivered given the operational capabilities of the firm and its supporting supply chain. The value proposition reflects the order winners, order qualifiers, and order losers for a key customer segment, and thus it greatly influences the competitive priorities for all the related operations across the supply chain. In making the translation from value proposition to competitive priorities, operations managers need to clearly specify what the operations management system must do well (key success factors), what it must do adequately, and what it must avoid doing (because it will jeopardize customer satisfaction and orders).

Outcomes and Value Proposition: Central to value proposition is the set of outcomes to be delivered by the firm and its supply chain. As recently noted by Melnyk et al. (2010),[10] supply chains are not simply cost driven; they are outcome driven. That is, all supply chains are built around six basic, major outcomes:

- *Cost*—Reducing price (initially) and cost (ultimately) is the key focus. Delivery and quality, while important, are secondary considerations and considered part of this outcome. It is important to recognize the difference between price and cost. Price focuses on what you pay for the good or service—it is the price found in the contract or on the tag. In contrast, cost represents all of the costs incurred including acquisition, storage, rework, and all other associated costs over the life of the product or services. As such, cost is a broader concept.
- *Responsiveness*—The ability to change quickly in terms of volume, mix, or location in response to changing conditions. Typically, responsiveness warrants a higher cost and price.
- *Security*—This involves supply chains that are safe and protected from external disruptions. Security is a relatively new requirement but has gained a great deal of attention recently, with cases of tainted food products from China and generic drugs from India.
- *Sustainability*—This outcome is different from security; it involves supply chains that are measuring and managing both environmental AND social dimensions.
- *Resilience*—This refers to supply chains that can deal with unexpected disruptive conditions or threats to supply, ranging from natural disaster to bankruptcies or even political embargos.
- *Innovation*—In recent years, many firms have increasingly relied on their supply chain as a source of product and process innovation. For example, IKEA long ago generated a com-

petitive advantage by changing how products were delivered. More recently, Procter & Gamble involved both suppliers and customers in its highly successful new "connect and develop" innovation process.

The most effective and sustainable supply chains are a blend of these outcomes—a blend that is attractive to the key customers (and for which these same customers are willing to pay) and that differentiates them in the minds of the customer. Achieving and delivering the desired blend of outcomes to the customer cannot be achieved by accident. It requires not only strategic planning and intent but also having the "right" supply chain and the "right" supplier base in place.

In reviewing these outcomes, it is important to recognize that, like the elements of value, not all the outcomes are equally important. Rather, recent research conducted by one of the authors has led to the finding that in mixing these outcomes, a 1–2–3 approach should be used. That is:

- One (1) of the outcomes must be critical. This forms the core of the firm's value proposition. It is that outcome that the firm will never compromise. It defines the essence of the firm and its supply chain.
- Two (2) of the outcomes are important. While not as critical as the prior outcome, they are important in that they describe how the outcomes will be delivered. These three describe the essence of the firm's value proposition and should include sustainability if the organization's view of sustainability is going to be more than public relations or waste management.
- Three (3, the remaining outcomes) are necessary. We do not have to do a great job on these outcomes; we simply need to be good enough.

Capabilities: The third element of delivering value is capabilities. Capabilities are unique and superior operational abilities that stem from the routines, skills, and processes that the firm develops and uses. Usually, abilities to deliver superior performance come from investments and developmental efforts in one or more of the following areas: processes, planning systems, technology, performance measurement, people and culture, and supply chain relationships.

Driving the effective and successful business model is the notion of "fit." That is, the highest level of value is delivered when what the key customer expects (order winners, order losers, order qualifiers) is addressed by the value proposition and delivered by the capabilities of the firm.

Value Added

If we were to focus only on value, we look at what something is worth to the key customer, independent of the costs (level of waste and impacts) incurred to provide this outcome. The concept of economic value added is well-known to most if not all business leaders, but this concept does not go far enough. To ensure that the pursuit of value is sensitive to the issues of total value generated and total waste, we use the concept of SVA, where:

Sustainable Value Added = (Level of Financial AND Environmental AND Social Value Generated) – Total Waste

The concept of total cost of ownership fits well with SVA. This more encompassing approach to value creation has been defined as the value that is created whenever benefits exceed costs.[11] Total waste, as used in this context, is the cost and is broader than the notion of waste previously introduced in this chapter. Within the context of S³CM, and rather than focusing only on economic waste alone, total waste includes attempting to value *all* social, environmental, and economic waste (our negative impact on the environment and people, relationships, suppliers, and customers). An example of this can be found in Puma's release of information regarding their environmental impacts from their own operations, and those of their tier-1 through tier-4 suppliers for water use, GHG emissions, land use, other air pollution, and solid waste with an associated cost of 145M EUR, or almost $192,000,000 US.[12] This transparency into environmental impacts is part of an Environmental Profit and Loss statement, also called an EP&L. While these valuations of environmental impact are not a full measure of the sustainable value added, they are a logical step in this direction and part of a movement toward integrated reporting and a new performance measurement frontier.

We already know that "brand" is a valuable asset. The Coca-Cola brand is worth more than half the company's market value, and a staggering 10 times the book value of its parent company.[13] If companies such as Coke or Microsoft can put brand on their books for umpteen billion dollars, what is the enhancement from more sustainable practices worth? When we start answering that question, then firms and their supply chains have a new opportunity to monetize the amount of value created from environmental and social actions as we move toward better performance metrics as indicators of sustainability and firm performance … or what we want you to start thinking about as SVA.

What this approach forces on management is the twin onus of sustainability—satisfying a real customer need while simultaneously reducing total waste. With this approach, we can see the limitations of prior approaches—at best, they focus on waste reduction and pollution prevention, and they do little for value maximization. The approach that forces management to focus on SVA is that of S³CM and value maximization—the third and highest level of the performance pyramid.

Sustainable Value Maximization

At this level of supply chain management, sustainability is integral to the business model.

That is:

- The key customer targeted is someone for whom sustainability (one of the six supply chain outcomes) is either an order winner or at a minimum an order qualifier.
- The value proposition explicitly identifies sustainability and offers it as something that the customer is willing to pay for.

- The firm has organized its capabilities to ensure that value is being delivered. This means that it focuses on both the maximization of value and the elimination of waste/pollution within the production system.
- Performance measurement enabled by systems thinking goes beyond the firm to include the supply chain and ultimately the community.

When viewed from this perspective, it becomes clear that environmental and social sustainability are integrated and simultaneously inclusive of business sustainability. This is the image that we see when we review the vision put forth by Polman for Unilever. It is a vision that emphasizes SVA; a vision that focuses on both value creation and waste reduction. It also represents a vision that seeks to ensure that the community benefits from sustainability—both as consumers and as suppliers. It also represents a situation where environmental and social sustainability is viewed as not only being critical for the firm and the planet but also essential to developing and maintaining a sustainable competitive advantage. For a synopsis of 20 studies showing the business case for sustainability, see "Sustainability Pays," a project by Natural Capitalism Solutions.[14]

Every firm should aim for these goals when developing a sustainable supply chain, and the rest of this book will focus on attaining these goals.

Summary

This is a book about developing and maintaining a strategic sustainable supply chain. Given the growing importance of sustainability, it is also important that we develop a thorough and well-grounded understanding of this business paradigm. That has been the goal of this chapter where we have made the following points:

- Sustainability can be implemented as waste management or as sustainable value management.

- When focusing on SVA, think in terms of the business model and strategy of the organization, value creation, and waste elimination.
- The business model forces us to think in terms of aligning three interrelated entities:
  - The key customer
  - The value proposition
  - The capabilities of the system
- We have chosen to focus on the notion of SVA, or value adjusted for waste. This approach has been used to force managers to recognize that they must deal with both the elements—value and waste.
- It is when we implement S³CM as sustainable value delivered that we see a system for synchronizing financial, environmental, and social sustainability.

Building on Chapter 3, we are now able to better understand the challenge of developing a sustainable supply chain. The next two chapters introduce performance measurement and tools.

Applied Learning: Action Items (AIs)—Steps You Can Take to Apply the Learning From This Chapter

AI: Does your organization currently value environmental or social aspects of functions?

AI: What is your business model: key customer, value proposition, and capabilities?

AI: How can you start measuring value creation and waste to enable the concept of SVA?

AI: What lean practices are in place within your organization?

AI: How would you explain to co-workers in other functions, or CFO why firms are putting a price on CO_2 emissions?

AI: How many and what types of waste are within your own operations?

Further Readings

Eccles, R. and A. Taylor. "The Evolving Role of Chief Sustainability Officers, Sustainable Business Practices." *Harvard Business Review* (2023). https://hbr.org/2023/07/the-evolving-role-of-chief-sustainability-officers.

Lovins, B., L. H. Lovins, and P. Hawkins. "A Roadmap for Natural Capitalism." *Harvard Business Review* 85 (2007): 7–8.

McKinsey & Co. *Resource Revolution: Meeting the World's Energy, Materials, Foods, and Water Needs.* Global Institute and Sustainability & Resource Productivity Practice, 2011.

McKinsey & Co. "Greenhouse Gas Abatement Cost Curves." Accessed December 11, 2024 at www.mckinsey.com/business-functions/sustainability-and-resource-productivity/our-insights/greenhouse-gas-abatement-cost-curves.

Whelan, T. and E. Douglas. "How to Talk to Your CFO About Sustainability." *Harvard Business Review* 99, no. 1 (2021): 86–93.

CHAPTER 5

Performance Measurement —Enabling Transparency, Visibility, and Sustainability

In God we trust; all others bring data.

—W. Edward Deming

Firms are now holding that entire supply chains are accountable for new performance metrics. Performance measurement and metrics are changing; consider the following:

- Walmart announced a goal to eliminate 20 million metric tons of GHG emissions from its global supply chain. This represents one-and-a-half times the company's estimated global carbon footprint growth for five years and is the equivalent of taking more than 3.8 million cars off the road for a year. Walmart's global supply chain footprint is many times larger than its operational footprint and represents a more impactful opportunity to reduce emissions.
- There is a Social Cost of CO_2 (SCC) that can be used to assess the impacts of GHG emissions and it has been in use for decades.[1] Additionally, over 30 percent of global GHG emissions have a price per ton put on them.[2]
- Puma released the world's first EP&L statement, uncovering 145M EUR of environmental impacts. Only 8M EUR were attributed to Puma's own operations, and the remaining 94 percent were within their tier-1 through tier-4 supply chain. The company says future developments for the EP&L initiative

include expanding the accounting methodology to include the social value created by the firm.

- The Science Based Targets initiative (SBTi) is a corporate climate action organization that enables companies and financial institutions to lead the way to a net-zero economy, innovate, and drive more sustainable growth by setting ambitious science-based emission reduction targets.
- Countries and regions worldwide have a myriad of standards and regulations impacting supply chains, including climate-related financial disclosure, circular economy initiatives, modern slavery legislation, and corporate sustainability reporting directives.

The growing complexity and changing landscape of sustainability are causing many to wait to see what metrics and standards will become accepted by the leading firms within an industry. Because these firms don't know what they will be measured and graded on, they don't know where to invest—so they wait. Those same organizations choosing to wait will inevitably have to catch up to proactive firms. For those willing to measure now (rather than waiting), numerous hidden opportunities await to better understand processes, align entire supply chains, and differentiate products and firms. Innovative firms are already taking a strategic stance on how they want to measure and manage sustainability opportunities. These early adopting firms provide insight that others can learn from and improve on. To help support this process, there are many metrics to help the next wave of adopting firms.

Objectives

1. Understanding the basics of performance measurement, including benchmarking, and how and where to integrate sustainability.
2. Review the performance measurement architecture including functions and types of metrics.
3. Review proactive versus outcome-based metrics.

Introduction

One of the most powerful management disciplines, the one that keeps people focused and pulling in the same direction, is to make an organization's purposes tangible. Managers do this by translating the organization's mission—what it, particularly, exists to do—into a set of goals and performance measures that make success concrete for everyone. This is the real bottom line for every organization—whether it's a manufacturer or a service provider. Its executives must answer the question, 'Given our mission, how is our performance going to be defined?[3]

Someone who has a lot to say about performance measurement, sustainability, and corporate performance (and whose views are in line with the quote that began this chapter) is Bob Willard. A review of Bob Willard's 2012's book *The New Sustainability Advantage* uncovers tangible performance improvements of innovative firms aligning mission and sustainability performance metrics. Based on years of working with an array of companies, Willard suggests that if a typical company were to use best-practice sustainability approaches already used by real companies, it could improve its profit by at least 51 to 81 percent within three to five years, while avoiding a potential 16 to 36 percent erosion of profits if it did nothing.[4] This business case is organized around seven bottom-line benefits that align with current evidence regarding the most significant sustainability-related contributors to profit. For example, a large manufacturer can:

1. Increase revenue by 9 percent.
2. Reduce energy expenses by 75 percent.
3. Reduce waste expenses by 20 percent.
4. Reduce materials and water expenses by 10 percent.
5. Increase employee productivity by 2 percent.
6. Reduce hiring and attrition expenses by 25 percent.
7. Reduce strategic and operational risks by 36 percent.

Given the evidence of improved performance, many managers are excited and cautious about where they should start and what should be measured. First things first, we must recognize that the lack of a widely accepted definition of S^3CM and the complexity of overlapping supply chains make the selection and use of metrics both difficult and increasingly important for strategic alignment. What is needed (and often overlooked) is a process that links the strategic imperative of sustainability to performance measurement and management and ultimately to corporate performance. This process must ensure alignment (consistency) between the various components so that what is done at one level is consistent with and supportive of the actions carried out at the other levels. A good starting point is understanding how you and your organization define sustainability.

Most firms start with the Brundtland definition of "meeting the needs of a current generation without compromising the needs of future generations to meet their own needs," and then add to this, customizing the meaning and keywords to align with their business model and a TBL. This broad definition is a starting place, but does not provide the necessary insight regarding how to measure and integrate sustainability within a company.

To better define what is important while also aligning mission and metrics, Bill Blackburn[5] suggests developing a model sustainability policy. This process starts with a statement combining the Brundtland definition with an IBL[6,*] and then adding a breakout of topics important to your firm. For example, a company commitment to sustainability could start with the vision: "It is in the interest of our company and society as a whole that our company moves along the path to sustainability. To that end, we will strive to achieve the following vision of performance." Anyone can customize this further to have three additional subareas of the vision covering financial capital, natural capital, and social capital. Within each of these areas, ask yourself the following questions:

- Do our business activities promote sustainable economic health for the company and global community?

---

*Also see Sroufe, (2018).

- Do we conduct our business in a manner that contributes to the well-being of our employees and society?
- Do we manage our operations in a way that protects the environment to ensure that the earth can sustain future generations and the company's ability to meet future needs?

By answering these questions and then looking for behaviors that support each of the three areas of the vision, you can further develop a customized sustainability policy to help guide behavior and measurement.[7] Operationalizing sustainability is a starting point for signaling what is important and how you will design performance metrics that influence behavior. Here is a sustainability policy created by a top ranked MBA sustainability programs students in class with one of the authors of this book:

Our vision of sustainable performance includes researching and developing business opportunities that are economically, environmentally, and socially beneficial.

- The program's economic success will depend on brand strength, community prosperity, and return on investment.
- Our social responsibility includes action-learning, working with corporations on the business case for sustainability, collaboration with communities, respect for stakeholders, systems thinking across disciplines, and an ethical approach to decision-making.
- Environmental responsibilities include resource conservation, reducing of supply chain impacts, systems thinking, recycling, closed-loop systems, the pursuit of energy efficiency, and renewable energy sources.

Corporate examples can be seen within FedEx's global citizens' report of the past and more recent global impact reports[8] and themes highlighting "delivering what tomorrow requires today," with goals to connect the world in responsible and resourceful ways, tracking progress in economics and access, environment and efficiency, community and disaster relief, people and the workplace. Others, such as UPS, are vague as to how sustainability is defined, instead stating their mission as "increase the efficiency and reduce the environmental impact of global commerce by combining the shipping activities of customers into a single, highly efficient logistics network." UPS translates this expertise into convenient services with a wide range of price points and delivery speeds, including options tailored to specific industries and expansion of carbon-neutral services to 36 countries.[9]

The vignettes at the start of this chapter and the FedEx and UPS examples highlight a few important trends. First, manufacturers and logistics providers alike are innovating practices and processes to meet the changing needs of their key customers and a diverse set of stakeholders. Sustainability policies are a starting point for signaling intentions with metrics signal what is important and what is not. This signaling is both within the firm, its supply chain and to the market as a whole. We also find firms taking on the sustainability challenge are already experiencing gains in financial, natural, AND social capital, the foundations of sustainability. Firms are doing this while generating SVA and strategic competitive advantage.

In this chapter, we propose that single-firm metrics overlook the opportunity to measure and plan for multifirm measures that are necessary to understand the performance of a supply chain. Example metrics include energy consumption, GHG emissions, and what is becoming a de facto measure within firms and across supply chains—CO_2. Next, we review a performance measurement architecture (Figure 5.1) and present evidence of the growth of sustainability performance metrics. We then go on to identify trends that will remain important to supply chain managers, and highlight the importance and differences of visibility and transparency now exposed within supply chains.

You Are What You Measure

Managers pursue multiple types of operations and supply chain metrics at different levels as a means to increase their visibility over aspects of the supply chain they do not control, yet know will have impact on their own company's performance. Leveraging the Chapter 4 business model to align key customers, capabilities, and value proposition provides any company an opportunity for process improvement. This improvement will rely upon applying metrics that enable

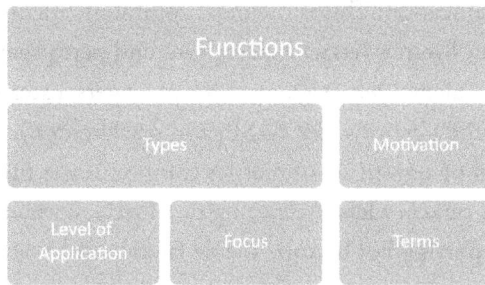

Figure 5.1 The performance measurement architecture

management to identify opportunities for improved profitability AND align sustainability objectives. The goal is to identify opportunities within an organization and across firms in a supply chain. We start with an understanding of the functions of performance measurement before transitioning to different types of metrics.

A metric is a verifiable measure assessed in both quantitative and qualitative terms and defined with respect to a reference point. This definition identifies several attributes of metrics.

- Metrics involve *measures* that capture data in numerical/quantitative form.
- Metrics are *verifiable*. Underlying the metric there should be a well-understood, documented process for converting data into the measure.
- Metrics require a *reference point*, otherwise known as a standard, providing a basis of comparison. Reference points are derived from previous performance, a computed or observed standard, or some ideal value (e.g., optimum value of performance).
- Metrics allow and encourage *comparisons* across processes, groups, time periods, and operating conditions.

Metrics exist because of, and to enable, people. They provide a language by which we can communicate specific information regarding the state or outcomes of a process. To understand their importance, consider the following functions provided by metrics:

- Communication: This is the most commonly identified function. Metrics report expectations and performance to process stakeholders (e.g., workers, managers, external agencies such as the GRI or CDP, SASB, and stockholders). Also, the selection of a given set of metrics communicates their importance to stakeholders. According to KPMG, corporate responsibility reporting has become the de facto law of business. Survey results show 95 percent of the Global 250 report corporate responsibility activities. What are you reporting/communicating?
- Control: Metrics enable managers to control and evaluate the performance of the people, processes, and business units. They also enable employees to control their own equipment and their own performance.
- Expectations: Metrics influence customers' expectations. For example, if we say that we will eliminate 20 million metric tons of GHGs by 2030, we have formed both an expectation and a metric (i.e., did we meet the amount proposed by the deadline?).
- Learning and Improvement: Metrics identify gaps between outcomes and expectations. Learning occurs when workers try to understand the causes of and remedies for these gaps.
- Transparency: Corporate reporting and transparency involves "the set of information items that relate to a firm's past, current, and future environmental and social management activities and performance ... [and their] financial implications."[10] Transparency is measured, managed, and reported by a firm and thus, the firm can control the message associated with its activities. Transparency is often revealed externally through corporate sustainability reports while following the GRI guidelines, and includes the submission of information to the CDP. Other innovative forms or transparency, enabled by technology, are helping firms to differentiate sustainability strategies. See, for example, trends in corporate responsibility reporting and the Dole Farm Locator Program.

Within the organic agriculture and food industry, Dole's Organic Farm Locator Program allows consumers to see where their food comes

Figure 5.2 Dole organic program farm #776

from and the farm and farmer who grew the fruit. With the help of a phone or your computer, you can now see Dole's supply chains with more transparency than ever before.

By utilizing the Dole Organic Farm Locator, (See Figure 5.2) you can find the Don Pedro farm in La Guajira, Colombia. Consumers can see that this banana farm has been certified since 2005, find photos of the farm, and certification Control Union Certification information from USDA—NOP Organic, ECC 834/2007 Organic, and Global GAP. Dole controls information and chain of custody communication to consumers knowing that organic credentials are important while providing access to all current and historical organic farm certifications. This emlerging form of transparency facilitates communication, sets expectations, and provides opportunities for consumers to learn more about the product and its supply chain. Consumers are now connected to supply chains and more willing to participate in the value-generation process.

- Visibility. Supply chain visibility is the ability of parts, components, or products in transit to be tracked from the manufacturer to their final destination. Visibility aims to improve and strengthen the supply chain by making data readily available to all stakeholders, including the customer. Supply chain visibility technology promotes quick response to change by allowing privileged users to take action and reshape demand or redirect supply. To take this a step further, organizations such as the United Nations Global Compact (UN GC) have a task force of industry partners to help identify common challenges and solutions to tracing products and raw materials through complex global supply chains. This traceability is part of the UNGC's current supply chain sustainability efforts.

With the ever-increasing amount of data available through tools such as LCA, new mapping technologies now provide more visibility into supply chains. Take, for example, Sourcemap.com (see Figure 5.3). This freeware site allows users to post LCA maps of products. Right now, you and anyone else can go to this website and see where a laptop comes from. A drill down into the LCA information can now tell customers or consumers what materials the product is made of, where these materials come from, and the amount of waste, for example, GHG emissions and CO_2 associated with manufacturing, transportation, use, and disposal or recycling of the product.

Managers can now use mapping and LCA information to identify the different entities and upstream and downstream linkages comprising the supply chain and value chain. In the abovementioned example, vanadium sourced from Kazakhstan contains 21.01 kg CO_2 with other sources of materials highlighted consisting of terbium, glass, bismuth, chromium, and mercury. A further breakdown of this information reveals summaries of CO_2 contributions from manufacture, transport, usage, end of life, and the delivered product. After the initial focus on which supply chain members are delivering, attention can turn to waste elimination and managing metrics with the greatest potential for increasing competitive advantage in terms of leveraging supply chain efficiency, product stewardship, innovation, and profitability.

Metrics play a critical role in translating an organization's strategy and business model into reality. They restate corporate objectives that are often broadly stated (e.g., reduce the impact of global commerce or increase market share) into actions that a person working in a given function (e.g., procurement) can understand. For instance, suppose a manufacturer wants to implement a strategy based on differentiating

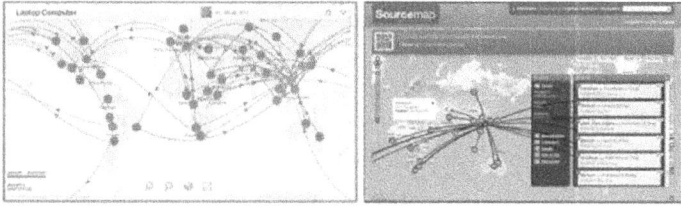

Figure 5.3 Sourcemap.com LCA laptop maps

products due to environmental attributes. One way to better define this goal for procurement is to measure the percentage of suppliers with third-party verification for their sustainability-related practices and product attributes. In addition, the supplier's ability to share information that now includes attributes of sustainability will reduce the risk of supply chain disruption. In this way, metrics define value and strategy in a business process. You can often get a better sense of a firm's value proposition by studying its metrics than you can be studying the corporate mission statement. Metrics and mission (the basis of the corporate value proposition) should be tightly linked to each other. As the adage goes, you are what you measure. Supply chains provide a dynamic opportunity to better understand how to leverage metrics within a systems-thinking mindset to enable sustainability. Metrics serve as strong proponents or strong impediments to value creation. Many managers believe that metrics are used only for control. In reality, metrics are used for communication and reporting outcomes, and in doing so, they also motivate action. When the elements of product value (cost, quality, and timeliness) are identified, quantified, and stated in the form of meaningful metrics, they become a powerful force for aligning organizational priorities, actions, and behaviors with strategic and value goals. If developed and implemented correctly, metrics form a critical link between value as it is strategically defined and the actions of various processes and people working within the operations management system. Metrics help to ensure that activities are consistent with what the firm wants to achieve in terms of value and how various employees will act.

Types of Metrics

Metrics are pervasive throughout different organizational levels and departments within a firm or supply chain. We will focus our attention on the different types of metrics found in most operations management systems (Table 5.1). These metrics can be categorized in four basic ways:

- Level of application: For what organizational levels are the metrics intended?
- Focus of the metrics: Are the metrics oriented toward efficiency or effectiveness?
- Terms of the metrics: Are the metrics stated in financial or operational terms?
- Motivation for the metrics: Are the metrics used in a predictive or outcome-oriented manner?

Level of Application

Generally, metrics can be applied at different levels or units of analysis.

The set of metrics used by top management should differ from those used by frontline workers. In some cases, however, the same metrics are applied at multiple levels. Metrics applied at higher organizational levels are often aggregates of lower-level metrics.

Focus of a Metric: Effectiveness Versus Efficiency

Effectiveness-based metrics measure performance on dimensions that are of greatest interest to targeted customers. These metrics answer the critical question, "What do I have to do well for the critical customer (and ultimately for the firm) to succeed?" Effectiveness-based metrics link customers, strategy, and activities together. In contrast, efficiency-based metrics focus more on resource utilization and costs. These measures are often formulated independent of customer considerations. Efficiency-based metrics answer the question, "How well or efficiently did I or my department do this task?" Both effectiveness and efficiency metrics are needed in operations and supply chain management.

Table 5.1 *Levels of metrics*[11]

Level	Examples	Orientation
Multifirm	Sustainable value added (SVA), economic value added (EVA),[9] risk of supply chain disruption, cradle-to-grave life cycle assessment (LCA), corporate ecosystem valuation (CEV),[##] shared value, Scope 3 GHG, normalized CO_2, Carbon Disclosure Project (CDP) supply chain member	Broad-based, strategic (long term) understanding of contribution from suppliers, own operations, to customers and end users; value, impact, and waste created in the system, includes traditionally overlooked externalities
Corporate or business unit	Sales, growth of sales, market share, stock prices, credit rating, performance on key strategic activities (e.g., on-time arrival and departure for Southwest Airlines), high-performance buildings (Leadership in Energy and Environmental Design [LEED], or Energy Star), Scopes 1 and 2 GHG, environmental profit and loss statement, included in Dow Jones Sustainability Index, FTSE 4 Good, MSCI	Broad-based, strategic (long term), aggregate units, many financial, includes recognition by external organizations
Product	Market share, contribution margin,[**] functionality, quality or reputation, repeat purchases, cost per unit (as compared to the budgeted cost), recommendations (by critical groups such as Consumer Reports, or Good Guide), inventory level, % of recycled content, free of xxx (where xxx could be an element such as Bisphenol A (BPA)), Energy Star, qualifies for Green Seal or Ecologo, Design for Sustainability, environmental product declaration (EPD), C2C certification	Broad-based, cross-functional, measure that can be measured at one location or across locations. Can be strategically oriented (e.g., market share, reputation, externally verified product attributes or labels, recyclability) or operational (e.g., inventory or design)

(Continued)

Table 5.1 (Continued)

Level	Examples	Orientation
Process	On-time delivery rate, number of units produced, lead time, zero waste, carbon neutral, water neutral, Scope 1 GHG emissions, 100% renewable energy	More focused, tactically oriented, stated in terms appropriate and meaningful to the function or group
Individual/ activity	Utilization, downtime, number of units produced per period; energy, water, or emissions per standard unit of production	Very focused, operational, emphasis on performance improvement, and normalized to unit of production

See the World Business Council for Sustainable Development (2024); www.wbcsd.org/.

** Contribution margin is defined as: price per unit—variable costs per unit. It is the amount of contribution each unit of sales makes toward offsetting fixed costs and, ultimately, toward attaining profit.

However, truly value-driven operations tend to elevate the importance of effectiveness metrics over efficiency metrics.

Metrics Stated in Financial or Operational Term

Management typically refers to supply chain performance metrics that focus on transportation attributes such as lead time, fill rate, or on-time delivery. Metrics are usually reported either in financial terms (e.g., return on investment, profitability, or other monetary measures) or operational terms (e.g., lead times, units of inventory, or number of defects).

Financial measures do not provide insight into how well business processes have performed, how effectively the supply chain has met the needs of critical customers, or how much waste can be attributed to supply chain processes. As was pointed out by Willard earlier in this chapter, sustainability leads to financial gains through increased productivity and revenue, while also decreasing energy, materials, attrition, risk, and waste.

Table 5.2 Puma EP&L statement (Phase I)

The environmental profit and loss							
EUR million	Water use	GH Gs	Land use	Other air pollution	Waste	Total	% of total
	33%	33%	25%	7%	2%	100%	
Total	47	47	37	11	3	145	100%
PUMA operations	<1	7	<1	1	<1	8	6%
Tier 1	1	9	<1	1	2	13	9%
Tier 2	4	9	<1	2	1	14	9%
Tier 3	17	7	<1	3	<1	27	19%
Tier 4	25	17	37	4	<1	83	57%

Source: Puma EP&L Press Kit.[†]

As noted in Chapter 4, waste is anything that does not add value to a product or service, such as, GHGs. Sustainability performance metrics such as GHGs are an opportunity for firms to realize a new level of waste measurement and associated costs as visibility increases within a supply chain. We have tools and standards enabling an understanding of where opportunities exist to decrease waste, while increasing competitiveness, customer value, and shareholder value[12] for firms across a supply chain. Knowing this, supply chain managers are measuring performance outside the firm, evaluating tier-1 through tier-4 suppliers, responding to stakeholders, and relying on third-party providers to help.

Operational metrics are most useful to those involved in carrying out a specific task or activity being measured because operational metrics can be linked to the sources of performance in the process. In contrast, financial metrics are useful for people who evaluate and compare processes (e.g., managers and investors). By putting things in monetary terms, financial metrics allow "apple-to-apple" comparisons.

New operational metrics include, but are not limited to, water use, GHG emissions, land use, air pollution, and waste. These new metrics helped form Puma's first EP&L statement.

[†]Puma has been doing this for over a decade, see for example, the Puma EP&L press kit (2011).

Puma is a sport-lifestyle company that designs and develops footwear, apparel, and accessories. Phase I of this three-phase process resulted in Puma uncovering and valuing environmental impacts in excess of 145M EUR (Table 5.2). This level of analysis included tier-1 through tier-4 suppliers and revealed that 94 percent of environmental impacts resulted from suppliers and not Puma's direct operations. Here we see new operational terms used to help link processes and performance while new trends toward integrated financial and sustainability reporting reveal efforts to measure environmental impacts and social value of a firm.

Motivation: Predictive and Outcome Metrics

Metrics can be used to judge outcome performance and predict future performance. An *outcome* metric supports evaluations of individuals and processes as a basis for rewards or for determining where attention is needed. For example, a manager's bonus might be tied to performance on a given set of metrics. In contrast, a *predictive* metric aims to increase the chances of achieving a certain objective or goal in the future. Predictive metrics are associated with aspects of the process that are thought to affect the outcomes of interest. If we are interested in reducing lead time, we might look at leading indicators of lead time such as the distance required to be traveled by an order, the current level of utilization in a process, and so on. Suppose new supply chain initiatives involve increasing social and natural capital. Then firms should implement communication and training programs to leverage existing certifications, collaboration with NGOs, and use a broad array of KPIs. Predictive metrics are appropriate when the interest is in preventing the occurrence of problems rather than correcting them.

In many systems, the bulk of metrics are outcome oriented, rather than predictive (Table 5.3). For example, they measure on-time delivery of products rather than looking at measures that might predict on-time performance (e.g., inventory accuracy, setup time, and total lead time for a specific operation). As a result, the metrics system gives the managers little information that suggests means for improvement. More and more, firms are turning their attention to developing predictive metrics. They recognize that such measures are far more useful. Some commonly used operational metrics include those in Table 5.3.

> *Measurement is the first step that leads to control and eventually to improvement. If you can't measure something, you can't understand it. If you can't understand it, you can't control it. If you can't control it, you can't improve it.*
>
> —H. James Harrington

What is the difference between predictive and outcome-based metrics? Experience (outcome-based metrics) is enlightening. It enables you to recognize a mistake when you make it again, and again, and again. Predictive metrics enable you to recognize a potential mistake before you make it. Predictive metrics are paramount to ensure the successful integration of sustainability into any firm.

Summary

We wanted to prominently place metrics within this book to emphasize what operations and supply chain systems should be considered for measuring. This helps to avoid organizations institutionalizing only what they are good at. Instead, S³CM provides an opportunity for a metrics evolution for some and a metrics revolution for others in changing how management plans for and delivers process performance. Metrics are communication! They must emphasize the mission of the organization and, in doing so, become a critical element within an organization as they make programs and processes concrete. Mission and metrics define everything we need to know.

This chapter started by highlighting vignettes of a changing performance metrics landscape. Next, best practice highlights showed significant improvements in revenue, energy, waste, water, and materials expenses, along with improvements in employee productivity, attrition, and strategic as well as operational risks. With improved performance as a goal, information then moved to discussing the functions, types, motivation, focus, and level of application of metrics. Within this

Table 5.3 Examples of predictive and outcome metrics

Performance category	Outcome metrics	Predictive metrics
Lead times	Total order to delivery lead time	Bottleneck cycle time Setup time Throughput time for longest process Number of steps in a process Distance in a process Inventory in the system
Flexibility	Number of product variants Percentage of products that are made to order	Number of different job classes (fewer is better) Number of levels in the typical bill of material Setup time Percentage of cross-trained employees Percentage of parts/components that are common across product line
Quality	Parts-per-million defective (PPM)	Number of certified suppliers Process capability (Cp, Cpk)
Cost	Unit cost variance (between standard and actual) Direct labor cost variances Direct material cost variances Overhead costs variances	Costs to date Number of steps in the process Distance traveled by the order Number of changes processed Throughput time
Morale and Teamwork	Number of labor disputes Grievances filed Number of employee-requested terminations Level of absenteeism	Number of suggestions per employee Amount of training/education time/employee Number of skills/person
Social capital	Number of minority-owned suppliers No child labor Unhealthy work environment Executive and board diversity	Level of diversity training Socially responsible supplier audits SA 8000 certification ISO 26000 certification Availability of Occupational Safety and Health Administration (OSHA) training Diversity hiring and promotion practices

(Continued)

Table 5.3 (Continued)

Perform ance category	Outcome metrics	Predictive metrics
	Nonrepresentation of women Transparency concern Corporate sustainability report Shared value	Women and minorities have at least four seats on the board and >5% of subcontracting Measure wide range of social and environmental performance metrics** Collaborate with NGOs (CDP, GRI, SASB, SBTi, WBCSD)
Natural Capital	Environmental fines (dollars) Pounds of pollution produced Percentage of waste recycled or reused Toxic Release Inventory (TRI) reporting Transport impacts of product and workforce Nonmonetary compliance sanctions Scopes 1–3 GHG emissions CEV	Process yield ISO 14000 and 50000 certifications Energy Star certifications Inventory of toxic materials on premises Percentage employees trained to handle toxic materials Floor space devoted to storage, processing, or disposal of toxic materials Investment in more efficient equipment Measure a wide range of indicators, including materials, energy, water, biodiversity, and LCA of product and transportation
DEI (Diversity, Equity, Inclusion)[13]	Hiring • Diversity of applicant pool • Diversity of hiring panel Representation Retention Advancement Leadership (% DEI focus) Suppliers (% DEI focus)	Job satisfaction and engagement Employee resource group (ERG) participation Accessibility

** As measured by S&P's ESG indicators of governance strengths as the effective reporting of a wide range of social and environmental performance metrics. Examples of social and natural capital metrics can be found in what was formerly known as KLD's indicators of environment, governance, and diversity. Measured and reported to socially responsible investors, researchers, and university students as either strengths or concerns of publicly traded firms.

context, trends regarding transparency and visibility showed more measurement and disclosure than at any time in prior history. This trend will only grow over time. To help align mission, metrics, and motivation, we focused on using predictive metrics to proactively avoid outcome-driven problems and create cost savings, knowing that cost avoidance and revenue generation would allow firms to leapfrog others in their industry. After reviewing applicable models, protocols, and standards, any organization can take a deep dive into performance measurement while considering outcome versus predictive metrics to customize an organization's sustainability assessment. There is room for improvement for any organization as supply chains integrate sustainability and performance measurement evolves to innovate, reduce waste, and maximize sustainable value.

Applied Learning: Action Items (AIs)—Steps You Can Take to Apply the Learning From This Chapter

AI: How many and what types of performance metrics do you use?

AI: How do you currently establish performance goals? Will this process be any different for natural or social capital?

AI: Identify sustainability performance metrics that will align with your existing mission.

AI: What predictive versus outcome metrics do you currently utilize?

AI: Run your business as if you did have to pay for carbon emissions, how would this change your approach to decision-making, management, and supply chain integration?

Further Readings

Blackburn, W. R. *The Sustainability Handbook.* Environmental Law Institute, 2016.

Busch, T. and P. Shrivastava. *The Global Carbon Crisis.* Bradford, United Kingdom: Greenleaf Publishing, 2011.

Eccles, R. G. and M. P. Krzus. *One Report-Integrated Reporting for a Sustainable Strategy.* Hoboken, NJ, New Jersey: Wiley, 2010.

Elkington, J. *The Zeronauts-Breaking the Sustainability Barrier.* Earthscan, 2012.

Elkington, J. *Green Swans: The Coming Boom in Regenerative Capitalism.* Greenleaf Book Group, 2020.

Hawken, P., ed. *Drawdown: The Most Comprehensive Plan Ever Proposed to Reverse Global Warming.* Penguin, 2017.

Henderson, R. M. "Reimagining Capitalism." *Management and Business Review* 1, no. 1 (2021).

Lovins, A., H. Lovins and P. A. Hawken. "A Road Map for Natural Capitalism." *Harvard Business Review*, July–August 2007.

Juniper, T. *What Has Nature Ever Done For Us?* London, UK: Profile Books, 2013.

Porter, M. E. and M. R. Kramer. "Creating Shared Value." *Harvard Business Review*, 2011.

CHAPTER 6

Sustainability—A Performance Measurement Evolution or Revolution, Models, and Programs

You never change things by fighting the existing reality. To change something, build a new model that makes the existing model obsolete.

—Buckminster Fuller

There are now models and programs available to help measure and manage sustainability initiatives:

- EPA SmartWay programs increase the availability and market penetration of fuel-efficient technologies and strategies that help freight companies save money while also reducing adverse environmental impacts. Specifically, SmartWay Transport programs lower emissions of CO_2, nitrogen oxides, and particulate matter. Since 2004, SmartWay Partners report: saving 397M barrels of oil ($52.3B in fuel costs saved); helping partners avoid 162M metric tons of CO_2—equivalent of taking over 16.7M cars off the road; eliminating 2.8M short tons of nitrogen oxides; and 114,000 short tons of particulate matter.
- The CDP's network of investors and purchasers represents over $100 trillion and works with global policymakers who use CDP data and insights to make better-informed decisions.
- The GRI with 14,000 reports from companies in over 1,000 countries provides the world's most widely used sustainabil-

ity reporting and disclosure standard. Additionally, over 60 countries and regions reference GRI in their policies. The GRI is an intrinsic element of integrated reporting, an initiative that combines the analysis and reporting of financial and nonfinancial performance annually in one report, see, for example Philips, Danon, SAP, Maersk, and DHL integrated reports.

There are several models, programs, guidelines, and examples of how firms have already started their development of S³CM. In this chapter, we expand on the context of performance measurement in Chapter 5, while exploring the existing enablers of the measurement and management of strategic sustainability initiatives.

Objectives

1. Understanding a performance hierarchy and the factors contributing to more comprehensive performance measurement
2. Introducing programs and guidelines to measure and manage supply chains
3. Reviewing key performance indicators providing insight for carriers and less-than-truck-load service providers

Sustainability: A Performance Measurement Evolution or Revolution?

We see financial and operational metrics as a performance hierarchy (Figure 6.1), with a typical progress of management thinking and strategic sustainability providing new opportunities to accelerate innovation. The ability to align sustainability as a strategic imperative across a supply chain means that you are simultaneously engaging multiple levels of the performance hierarchy, from cost savings to value creation while using sustainability as a catalyst for integrating new multifirm performance metrics. With increased scrutiny of investors and customers, coupled with the ability of technology to quickly showcase supply chain problems, multifirm metrics aligning sustainability provide insight for risk management. This level of thinking also enables both visibility and transparency through telling compelling stories of

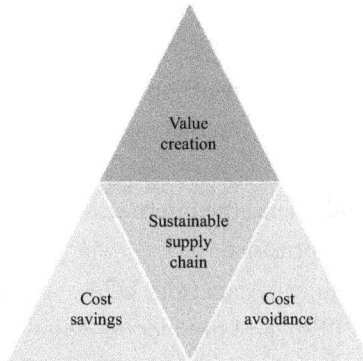

Figure 6.1 Performance hierarchy

efficiency, stakeholder engagement, and innovation. Companies are now mapping and managing supply chains in new ways.

In order for management to understand the interrelationships between corporate and supply chain performance, broad-based measures are required to move firms from efficiency and cost savings into opportunities for innovation, revenue generation, and new markets. While we worry about second- and third-tier suppliers, and their negative externalities, we know that technology, that is, big data analytics, Internet of Things (IoT), and Generatie Artificial Inteligence (GenAI), is enabling all that we discussed about in Chapter 2 regarding systems integration and better decision making. We know for very large firms, you cannot manage the entirety of the supply chain. Yet, we can focus on managing key suppliers and performance metrics. When doing this in the context of the third edition S³CM books, we are trying to get readers to take a holistic view of opportunities and relationships. As the sustainability paradigm evolves, our business acumen has changed to embrace a more dynamic systems perspective. Metrics now integrate financial and nonfinancial performances. The complexity of the supply chain requires a different approach to understanding how and where sustainability will align with your business model and corporate performance. Several factors contributing to the need for more comprehensive performance management include but are not limited to:

- The push for more visibility and transparency within supply chains
- The increasing complexity of supply chains
- The need to go beyond internal metrics to understand a supply chain perspective
- The need to understand the interrelationships of corporate *and* supply chain performance
- The new availability of data from LCA, environmental product declarations (EPDs), and product development processes
- Pandemics and learning from COVID-19 disruptions
- The use of new performance metrics for supply chain analysis and optimization.
- The need for accountability of supply chain waste and SVA
- Differentiation, story telling, and competitive advantage

Managers need to look into their supply chain by measuring and comparing the performance and activities of companies they do not directly control. Increased visibility and shared metrics assist management with the integration, synchronization, and optimization of processes cradle to grave (raw material extraction to landfill) or C2C (from raw materials to closed-loop systems recapturing raw materials as inputs). Implementing a supply chain strategy requires metrics that align performance with the objectives of other members of the supply chain. Supply chain and sustainability managers need to work collaboratively to generate the greatest mutual gains through resource efficiency and risk management. Aligned metrics help shift management's attention to making decisions that also align with the goals of the entire supply chain.

The overlay of sustainability within supply chain analysis and planning involves an understanding of how to approach creating sustainable value, and the application of emerging measurement tools and quantitative models that characterize various relationships and economic synergies in the supply chain. The field of supply chain analysis/optimization has made significant strides in both theoretical and practical applications of waste reduction. The application of a sustainability lens to analysis results in an unprecedented mixture of predictive and outcome models, global reporting, new visibility, and transparency within supply chains. Much like the Puma EP&L example, the ability to quantify full costs of operations, products, and supply chains is only growing in importance. Analysis and optimization are now being extended to reduce social sustainability issues. Next, we discuss how to get started, and the guidelines, tools, and models already available to leverage the integration of strategic sustainability into supply chain management.

Models, Programs, Guidelines, and Tools to Help Integrate Sustainability

In this chapter, we are building on a foundation for understanding performance metrics reviewed in the previous chapter while foreshadowing sustainability as the driver of a performance revolution. We introduce proven models, practices, and insight that help guide measurement and process improvement. The information presented here briefly summarizes models, programs, guidelines, and tools to help customize your own integration opportunities and processes.

The Supply Chain Operations Reference Model

For many, starting with a thorough understanding of your supply chain sets the foundation for integrating sustainability initiatives. With the advent of supply chain management, managers have increasingly sought to coordinate activities spanning customer and supplier organizations. One of the challenges of this approach is finding new ways to communicate objectives and performance outcomes among supply chain partners. In the late 1990s, a group of industrialists from about 70 leading companies created an organization called the "Supply Chain Council." Working together, they developed the Supply Chain Operations Reference Model (commonly known as the SCOR model).[*] The model

---

[*] See https://majorsustainability.smeal.psu.edu/greenscor-model/#:~:text= GreenSCOR:%20The%20New%20and%20Improved,foster%20sup- ply%20chain%20value%20creation for more information on the Green SCOR model.

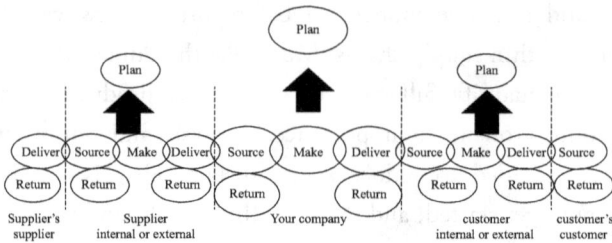

Figure 6.2 The SCOR model and its major components

was originally conceived as a framework reference defining concepts and metrics that could be used by organizations in any industry segment to share information with supply chain partners.

The SCOR model includes more than just metrics; it illustrates tools for mapping and describing supply chain processes (see Figure 6.2). It also describes supply chain management best practices and technology. SCOR best practices section includes environmentally responsible supply chain management (called GreenSCOR). However, we will focus here on several dimensions and relative metrics of the model. The SCOR model identifies basic management practices at different levels of operation. For example, "level 1" processes include Plan, Source, Make, Deliver, and Return. One of the basic tenets of the SCOR model is that metrics should cascade hierarchically from one level to the next.

At each level addressing the supply chain, SCOR addresses five basic dimensions of performance. They are:

- Supply Chain Delivery Reliability:
  - The performance of the supply chain in delivering the correct product, to the correct place, at the correct time, in the correct condition and packaging, in the correct quantity, with the correct documentation, and to the correct customer.
- Supply Chain Responsiveness:
  - The velocity at which a supply chain provides products to the customer.
- Supply Chain Flexibility:
  - The agility of a supply chain in responding to marketplace changes to gain or maintain competitive advantage.

- Supply Chain Costs:
    - The costs associated with operating the supply chain.
- Supply Chain Asset Management Efficiency:
    - The effectiveness of an organization in managing assets to support demand satisfaction. This includes the management of all assets: fixed and working capital.

The SCOR model identifies performance metrics for each of these dimensions. One of the model's objectives is to provide a framework for benchmarking and for translating strategy into practice. The following strategic environmental metrics allow the SCOR model to be used as a framework for environmental accounting:

- CO_2 emissions (tons CO_2 equivalent)
- Air pollutant emissions (tons or kg)
- Liquid waste generated (tons or kg)
- Solid waste generated (tons or kg)
- Recycled waste (percent)

The SCOR framework ties emissions to the originating processes, providing a structure for measuring environmental performance and identifying where performance can be improved. The model's hierarchical nature allows strategic environmental footprint goals to be translated to specific targets and activities. The evolution of the SCOR model now includes social impact considerations in supply chain analysis. For each supply chain function in SCOR, careful consideration is given to social and environmental risks and opportunities.[†] The results of mapping a supply chain and benchmarking analysis provide the level of performance necessary to be on par with the industry middle performers and levels required to gain differential advantage. The benchmarking data can indicate the impact of improvement in a given outcome performance metric on revenues, costs, or investments. This type of analysis

---

[†]Upgrading the SCOR Model to include Social and Environmental Factors; accessed at https://majorsustainability.smeal.psu.edu/greenscor-model/ #:~:text=GreenSCOR:%20The%20New%20and%20Improved,foster%20supply%20chain%20value%20creation.

helps partners in a supply chain to plan and prioritize sustainability improvement initiatives following an overall business strategy.

The primary benefit cited by users of models like this includes process metrics and the benchmarks included in the SCOR guidelines. These guidelines help show company executives a tangible picture of supply chain gap analysis and shortcomings, helping to direct supply chain performance plans.

Global Reporting Initiative (GRI)

The GRI (www.globalreporting.org/) is a multistakeholder nonprofit organization founded in the United States in 1997 by the Coalition of Environmentally Responsible Economies (CERES). In 2002, GRI was formally inaugurated as a United Nations Environment Program (UNEP) collaborating organization and moved its central office to Amsterdam, where the Secretariat is currently located. GRI has regional "Focal Points" in Australia, Brazil, China, India, the United States, and South Africa, and a worldwide network of 30,000 members from NGOs and businesses.

This organization produces a sustainability reporting framework that has become the de facto framework used around the world to enable greater organizational transparency. Its guidelines are available to the public at no cost. GRI's reporting guidelines are used by thousands of companies in 90 different countries.[‡] The GRI's mission is to mainstream the disclosure of environmental, social, and economic performance metrics for companies. The GRI aims to develop a standard practice for sustainability reporting that allows stakeholders to compare sustainability-related data. These guidelines have been in use for years since the original set of GRI reporting guidelines was released in 2000 and updated several times.

[‡]The Global Reporting Initiative (GRI) produces a comprehensive Sustainability Reporting Framework that is widely used around the world, to enable greater organizational transparency. The Framework, including the Reporting Guidelines, sets out the Principles and Indicators that organizations can use to report their economic, environmental, and social performance. GRI is committed to continuously improving and increasing the use of the guidelines, which are freely available to the public. www.globalreporting.org/about-gri/.

There are several options for reporting depending on the level of detail and amount of metrics a firm can measure and verify. After a company has decided to utilize the GRI reporting structure, the GRI metrics can be used as an audit template internally. The internal auditing and reporting process categorizes information for a general profile disclosure, a management approach, an executive mission statement, and a strategy for executing sustainable initiatives. These *initiatives* are then linked to performance indicators as they relate to economic, environmental, and social metrics. The principles and guidelines help tailor the report to a company's specific industry and the sustainability challenges they face.

Primary benefits of GRI reporting include using existing performance metrics for environmental, social, and human rights, society, product responsibility, and the ability to have third-party verification of report contents. Thus, you do not have to reinvent the wheel when looking for relevant environmental and social metrics. Developing the GRI 2021 Standards-based materiality matrix and sustainability report can be a beneficial undertaking for any company. The auditing and reporting process facilitates process-level understanding of operations and supply chains. It should be leveraged to inform management decisions, and identify activities and benchmarks for cost reduction and avoidance, supply chain integration, brand reputation, and market differentiation. GRI guidelines and performance metrics are also leveraged to assess corporate governance and companies such as combined with the annual financial reports (see, e.g., Novo Nordisk, United Technologies, PepsiCo, Southwest Airlines, Bayer, and Philips). KPMG found that over 90 percent of G250 firms report sustainability performance.[1] One reason for the increase in reporting, in a survey of GRI report readers, 90 percent of those polled said that reading sustainability reports resulted in them viewing the companies in a more positive light.[2]

Carbon Disclosure Project (CDP)

In 2000, the CDP (www.cdp.net) was established to collect information from companies to "accelerate unified action on climate change." Based in the United Kingdom, the CDP provides centralized accounts of corporations' climate-change and water-management policies and measures their direct impact on the environment through GHG emissions. Working with over 740 institutional investors holding over $136T in assets, the CDP has an expansive worldwide presence spanning 50 locations, including offices in New York, Berlin, Sao Paulo, Beijing, and Tokyo.

CDP reports a company's emissions based on scope, reduction from base year, and target year emissions. Like many sustainability programs, CDP believes in using base targets to set goals for reduction. In the supply chain public procurement options, supplier companies' carbon information is requested to identify emissions through all parts of the production and distribution process. *The Supply Chain Report, A New Era: Supply Chain Management in a Low-Carbon Economy* survey results of CDP reporting organizations and suppliers.[3] Results of the survey show that 90 percent of CDP supply chain member organizations have a climate change strategy. In addition, 62 percent reward suppliers for good carbon management practices with 39 percent soon to deselect suppliers that do not adopt such measures. A recent *CDP Global Supply Chain Report* found that businesses must acknowledge that their environmental impact extends beyond their direct operations, and that climate change and nature are not being tackled together despite growing awareness of the benefits of addressing them holistically.[§] The CDP also collects data outside of carbon management. Water-intensive companies report water usage and issues regarding coping with threats arising from water scarcity, pollution, and flooding. Cities report in order to prepare for effects of climate change, benchmark, and relate to the business communities.

To begin disclosing, a company submits an online questionnaire focusing on targets, emissions, risk management, scope, and so on, This

---

[§]See this report at https://dfge.de/cdp-global-supply-chain-report-2022/.

can be done individually, or the CDP offers links to carbon calculator partners, consultancy partners, and third-party verification partners. The resulting reports (see Figure 6.3) allow you to calculate a carbon footprint, identify areas for improvement, and benchmark against other groups.

There are a number of benefits associated with reporting emission data and water use data through the CDP. One key benefit is the opportunity to advertise successes, particularly compared to industry competitors.

Reporting this data can also help an organization identify areas for improvement in energy efficiency and cost savings. Organizations benefit by having prepared a standardized response for investor inquiries regarding emissions and water use. In addition, participation in the CDP can be viewed as a favorable demonstration of transparency that can help set an organization apart from its competitors. This can be of particular value when investor confidence in the integrity of organizations is wavering.

Greenhouse Gas (GHG) Protocol

While climate change policy is evolving, organizations are seizing the GHG space as a means of differentiation and waste reduction. To help in this process, the GHG Protocol Initiative (www.ghgprotocol.org) arose when the World Resources Institute (WRI) and World Business Council for Sustainable Development (WBCSD) recognized the need for an international standard for corporate GHG accounting and reporting. Together with multinational corporate partners such as British Petroleum and General Motors, WRI identified an agenda to address climate change, among which included the need for standardized measurement of GHG emissions. In the late 1990s, WRI and WBCSD convened a core steering group comprising members from environmental groups (WWF, Pew Center on Global Climate Change, The Energy Research Institute) and from industry (Norsk Hydro, Tokyo Electric, Shell) to engage in a multistakeholder standards development process.

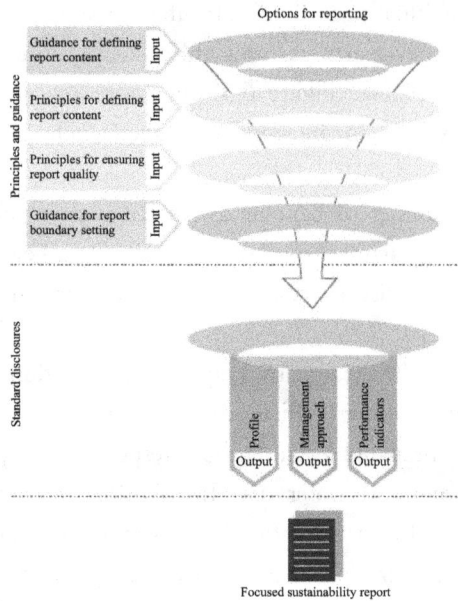

Figure 6.3 The GRI structure—the major components

The GHG Protocol is now the most widely used international accounting tool for government and business leaders to understand, quantify, and manage GHG emissions. As part of a decade-long partnership between the WRI and the WBCSD, the GHG Protocol is the result of work with businesses, governments, and environmental groups worldwide to build a new generation of credible and effective programs for tackling climate change. It serves as the foundation for nearly every GHG standard and program in the world—from the International Standards Organization (ISO) to The Climate Registry—and hundreds of GHG inventories prepared by individual companies. The GHG Protocol also offers developing countries an internationally accepted management tool to help their businesses compete in the global marketplace and their governments make informed decisions about climate change.

The GHG Protocol was published in 2001. Since then, the GHG Protocol has developed a suite of tools to assist companies in calculating their GHG emissions and additional guidance documents such as the GHG Protocol for Project Accounting. Additionally, WRI and WBCSD have partnered with governments, businesses, and NGOs in both developed and developing countries to promote the broad adoption of the GHG Protocol as the foundation for climate change strategies.

The primary benefits of using the GHG Protocol include its acceptance as a global standard, understanding of process-level performance metrics, and the scope and bounds of GHG measurement for organizations and supply chains. This information is important for understanding and determining who is responsible for GHG emissions, goal setting, and differentiating from others within an industry. Understanding starts with knowing the scope of GHG emissions and what you have direct control over.

GHG Protocol Emission Definitions

Scope 1: Direct GHG emissions occur from sources that are owned or controlled by the company (e.g., emissions from combustion in owned or controlled boilers, furnaces, vehicles) along with emissions from chemical production in owned or controlled process equipment.

Scope 2: Electricity-indirect GHG emissions account for GHG emissions from the generation of purchased electricity consumed by the company. Purchased electricity is defined as electricity that is purchased or otherwise brought into the organizational boundary of the company. Scope 2 emissions physically occur at the facility where electricity is generated.

Scope 3: Other indirect GHG emissions are an optional reporting category that allows for the treatment of all other indirect emissions. Scope 3 emissions are a consequence of the activities of the company, but occur from sources not owned or controlled by the company. Some examples of Scope 3 activities are extraction and production of purchased materials; transportation of raw materials and finished goods; and use of sold products and services. For products such as consumer electronics, the use of the product will have the largest impact on GHG emissions.

The ISO adopted the GHG Protocol Corporate Accounting and Reporting Standard as the basis for its ISO 14064: Specification with Guidance at the Organization Level for Quantification and Reporting of GHG Emissions and Removals. This milestone highlighted the role of the GHG Protocol's Corporate Standard as the international standard for corporate and organizational GHG accounting and reporting. ISO, WBCSD, and WRI signed a Memorandum of Understanding to jointly promote both global standards. The SCOR model, CDP, and GHG Protocol provide vast amounts of information for global supply chain mapping, benchmarking, and performance metrics. These initiatives are broad-based, providing organizations with proven guidelines and models for measuring, understanding, and, with the help of the GRI framework, reporting process-level performance rolled up into organizational and supply chain performance. Two of the three initiatives are specifically focused on GHG and CO_2 measurement. What many supply chain service providers need at a more micro level includes incentives, policy, and technical solutions to optimize transportation networks in a company's supply chain. Thus, we next introduce programs within a U.S. context for fuel efficiency and waste reduction.

The SmartWay Program

As we found with the Puma EP&L example, many manufacturers have found that a significant portion of their carbon footprint lies in the supply chain and distribution of products. To help reduce these impacts and better manage your supply base, you can leverage existing collaborative efforts from the SmartWay Program (http://www.epa.gov/smartway). This is the U.S. EPA's program for improving fuel efficiency and reducing GHGs and air pollution from the transportation supply chain industry. The program includes general areas of focus: transport partnership, tractors and trailers, finance, and technical assistance. Developed jointly by the EPA and Charter Partners that were represented by industry stakeholders, environmental groups, American Trucking Associations, and Business for Social Responsibility, the program was launched over two decades ago. SmartWay comprises partnerships, financial incentives, policy and technical solutions, and research and evaluation projects that find new ways to optimize the transportation networks in a company's supply chain. To date, the partnership includes nearly 4,000 companies and associations committed to improving fuel efficiency. The SmartWay Programs support the supply chain industries in the following ways:

- The SmartWay Partnership Program is a government/industry collaboration between EPA, freight shippers, carriers, logistics companies, and other stakeholders to *voluntarily* achieve improved fuel efficiency and reduce environmental impacts from freight transport.
- Participating companies benchmark their current freight operations; identify technologies and strategies to reduce carbon emissions, track emissions reductions, and project future improvement.
- SmartWay partners demonstrate to their customers, clients, and investors that they are responsible for the emissions associated with goods movement, are committed to CSR and sustainable business practices, and are reducing their carbon footprint.
- SmartWay-endorsed tractors and trailers meet voluntary equipment specifications that can reduce fuel consumption by 10 to 20 percent for newer long-haul tractors and trailers. Each qualified tractor/trailer combination can save operators between 2,000 and 4,000 gallons of diesel per year while also reducing GHG emissions and air pollutants.
- To help with capital expenditures, programs include helping companies acquire fuel-efficient emission reduction technologies through easier access to financial mechanisms such as reduced-interest loans with flexible terms.
- To provide evidence-based solutions, the SmartWay assessment program tests and verifies emissions reductions and fuel savings from various available technologies, such as tractor and trailer aerodynamics, auxiliary power units, and wide-based tires. As a result, companies can compare the fuel efficiency and environ-

mental performance of various technologies and make more informed purchases.

Benefits from becoming a SmartWay partner starts with the assessment of freight operations; calculating fuel consumption and carbon footprint; and tracking fuel efficiency along with emission reductions annually. In exchange for this upfront learning and resource expenditure, the EPA ranks and publicizes partner's performance on the SmartWay Partner List. Superior performers earn the SmartWay Partner logo and associated point value. Participation in SmartWay helps carriers to identify opportunities to improve efficiency; demonstrate efficiency to potential customers; and reduce fuel costs. Participation in Smart-Way also helps shippers and logistics companies choose more efficient carriers; assess optimal mode choices; and reduce their transport carbon footprint.

The SmartWay programs provide a focused insight into fuel and pollution reduction that for many invokes an image of long haul tractors and trailers. It is also beneficial to drill down into more detail regarding a GHG focus within carriers and the less than truckload (LTL) service providers. This insight reveals several existing practices with room for many in the industry to catch up to best practices. After reviewing activities within a regional context for logistic service providers, we next transition into information on how corporate sustainability professionals perceive successful sustainability initiatives and how these same professionals work with supply chain professionals to collaborate for success.

GHG Management Within Carriers and an LTL Company Context

Suppliers of both goods and services to leading-edge sustainable organizations are seeing a shift from *optional* GHG improvement initiatives to *required* sustainability strategies to remain a viable supply chain partner. The first step in S³CM for most organizations is to measure and control direct and indirect GHGs in-house, or what is generally referred to as sources owned and controlled by the company (Scope 1 direct emissions) and those from electricity consumed by a firm (Scope 2 indirect emissions). However, for many manufacturers, a significant portion of their carbon footprint lies in the supply chain and distribution of products. More aggressive sustainability programs now expand their assessment and improvement requirements to Scope 3 partners.

PITT OHIO

SUPPLY CHAIN ▪ GROUND ▪ LTL ▪ TL

PITT OHIO—Transportation solutions provider

Specifically, one of the largest contributors of CO_2 for many manufacturers' total carbon footprint is the logistics services required to properly position material and finished products in today's global supply chains. Despite the relatively large contribution of transportation to an overall carbon footprint, one of the major hurdles in tracking supply chain emissions is understanding how to develop Scope 1 through Scope 3 emissions reporting capabilities.

The leadership of some carriers such as PITT OHIO, recognizes both the need and the potential benefit of gaining visibility and control over their carbon footprint as important to maintaining their competitive advantage in the industry into the future. This case example describes the elements of measuring CO_2, can provide the necessary link to current activity-based costing (ABC) systems to permit viable CO_2 allocation to customers, and reveals best practices to assist any carrier in developing a strategic sustainability plan.

LTL Carbon Metrics

The GHG Protocol Corporate Standard provides internationally accepted guidance for companies and other organizations preparing a GHG emissions inventory. It covers the accounting and reporting of the six GHGs covered by the Kyoto Protocol—CO_2, methane (CH_4), nitrous oxide (N_2O), hydrofluorocarbons (HFCs), perfluorocarbons (PFCs), and sulfur hexafluoride (SF6). While all six gases are not emitted from every industry, the guidance provides a structured approach to identifying scope bounds for an emission inventory and a science-based methodology for summarizing an overall CO_2 equivalent. The protocol was designed with the following objectives for all firms including transportation providers:

- To help companies prepare a GHG inventory that represents a fair account of their emissions using standardized approaches and principles.
- To simplify and reduce the costs of compiling a GHG inventory.
- To provide businesses with information that can be used to build an effective strategy to manage and reduce GHG emissions.
- To increase consistency and transparency in GHG accounting and reporting among various companies and GHG programs.

The protocol builds on the experience and knowledge of leading experts from businesses, NGOs, governments, and accounting associations. It has been road-tested by companies in multiple countries. The GHG Protocol Initiative's vision is to harmonize GHG accounting and reporting standards internationally to ensure that different trading schemes and other climate-related initiatives adopt consistent approaches to GHG accounting.

Preparing an emission inventory has the potential to be straightforward in some environments where only direct emissions are calculated. The aggregation, transfer/sortation, line haul, and distribution nature of LTL and parcel transport add complexity to CO_2 calculation and distribution not encountered in bulk transportation methods. Multiple types of equipment in various sizes, picking up and delivering shipments with a wide variety of sizes, weights, and distances traveled make it a challenge to determine exactly how much CO_2 is generated within each step of a process, and even more challenging to calculate what portion of that carbon footprint belongs to each stakeholder involved.

Carbon Assessment

With the insight provided by PITT OHIO customers and a number of these companies in the early stages of measuring supply chain CO_2 emissions, one of the authors helped this company with a carbon assessment. They have goals and performance metrics tied to CO_2. Carrier selection is moving toward a carrier's ability to reduce CO_2, and the three primary decision criteria for some customers are a combination of service, price, and sustainability, not necessarily in this same order.

One of the primary opportunities to get started is a baseline CO_2 assessment (see Figure 6.4). After reviewing several publicly available carbon calculators, we find these approaches to be oversimplified by looking only at average burn rates and load factors, they aggregate all trucking for LTL and TL, or they do not produce the same numeric results. They will make any assessment difficult to defend as the results will not be customized. A benchmarking of existing calculators revealed an opportunity for a customized assessment solution while leveraging existing internal data.

Enabling PITT OHIO's ability to draw from multiple sources of GHG emission data, coupled with the support of personnel, and based on best-in-class practices, a customized carbon calculator was created and recently received a patent.[¶] When developing calculators, tools, and dashboards like this, we propose taking a Scope 1 and Scope 2 assessment model based on calendar year of data. The bounds for this CO_2 assessment should include the electricity, natural gas, propane, and fuel oil used at the facility level. To give you an idea of the scale of this approach, this baseline assessment for PITT OHIO assessed over 20 terminals across nine states; using B-5 diesel fuel for over 700 tractors and over 400 straight trucks; gasoline consumption for 60 nonrevenue fleet vehicles; and all airline miles.

The insight gained during this assessment reveals over 125,000 metric tons of CO_2 associated with PITT OHIO operations. It's no surprise that tractors and straight trucks impact 90 percent of the firm's CO_2 footprint. Electricity consumption at the terminals is the next

[¶]See https://pittohio.com/myPittOhio/news/2024/pitt-ohio-receives-patent-for-carbon-emissions-calculations.

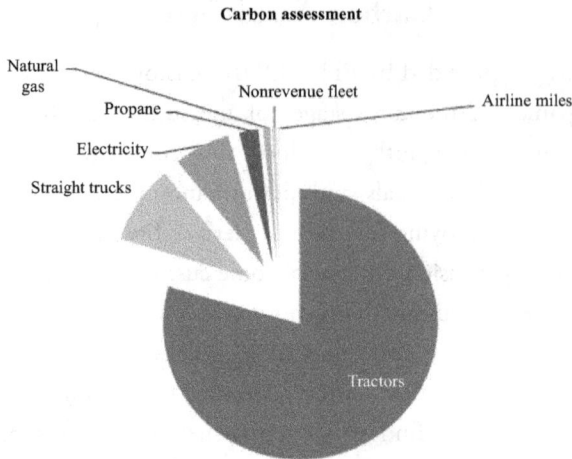

Figure 6.4 PITT OHIO—*carbon assessment generated by its carbon calculator*

largest contributor followed by propane and then natural gas. Collecting the location-level utility and fleet data is a good exercise in leveraging existing performance management and environmental management systems. This process will help to uncover gaps in the data. Existing programs and efforts to reduce impacts at terminals have gone a long way toward resource efficiency for many common facilities initiatives throughout the industry such as electricity and water conservation. Programs to reduce fuel consumption within fleet vehicles is a step in the right direction, yet more attention can be put on tractors and straight trucks as a percentage reduction in fuel consumption will have proportionally larger CO_2 reductions.

As an LTL service provider, PITT OHIO is in the business of moving customer's goods with high service rates and competitive pricing. To drill deeper into the CO_2 assessment to look for understanding and opportunities for new services, any company will next want to look at the customer's portion of an LTL's CO_2 footprint.

Customer's Portion of LTL'S Carbon Footprint

Utilizing the existing activity-based costing system and insight from management, we collaboratively developed and assessed a CO_2

equivalent on a per-shipment basis for clients. Based on data, and several discussions with management, the agreed-upon best approach for the allocation of CO_2 to a customer can be based on distance, weight, and cube while utilizing a CO_2 emission coefficient for B-5 diesel fuel from soy-based and low-sulfur sources. Based on customer data, per-trip amounts of CO_2 can be generated and rolled up into a monthly amount of emissions in-line with what some customers are already asking for. Customer allocation also provides an opportunity for offering "carbon-neutral" options for shipments that other providers such as FedEx and UPS are already selling to their customers.

The information and insight from a CO_2 inventory assessment project like this provide opportunities to better understand and leverage natural capital through outcome metrics while working toward predictive metrics, GRI reporting, and certifications. KPIs for assessing the impact of future sustainability initiatives typically start with natural capital and CO_2 and become more nuanced when assessing social capital. These opportunities for differentiation capture short-term positioning of information and analysis capabilities with the growing need for more transparency and better measurement of sustainability initiatives. We next summarized benchmarking regarding important sustainability factors in the LTL industry that align with natural capital, specifically looking at CO_2 emissions and resource efficiency.

Carrier and LTL Carbon Management Best Practices

Current commitment to managing and improving the carbon footprint of members of the supply chain's transportation segment varies significantly across the industry. Some LTL service providers show no evidence that they have taken any steps to track or manage their carbon footprint. Marketing material, websites, and strategic plans rarely acknowledge the concept of sustainability as important to the industry or their customers providing a short-term window of opportunity for differentiation and possibly competitive advantage.

Most regional LTL carriers have some evidence of interest in impacting natural capital. Few reference membership in the EPA's SmartWay Transport Partnership as an indicator of natural capital. In some cases, the SmartWay logo on promotional material and websites is the only recognition given to natural capital. Other carriers provide lists of environmental impact reduction initiatives, most of which include: recycling, idle and speed controls, and low-emission fuels.

A review of the LTL web landscape finds few LTL carriers presenting natural or social capital as a strategic initiative. Table 6.1 provides a list of the various techniques and practices that LTL carriers are promoting as indicators of natural capital. The first section of this list identifies the most commonly identified CO_2 reduction initiatives. However, most, if not all, would also be considered good business decisions as they reduce costs AND improve service. Also listed are those CO_2 reduction practices of the more environmentally proactive carriers.

Expanding the search to larger carrier groups and other modes uncovers a number of "Differentiating Strategic" sustainable practices. Most large transportation companies do not acknowledge the common activities listed previously as part of their sustainability programs. It is implied that they are doing all of those things and they have moved on to more strategic initiatives. From Old Dominion's inclusion of electric, natural gas, and hybrid vehicles to UPS's carbon-neutral program, most of the larger and multimodal carriers are going beyond basic efficiency improvements. Table 6.2 identifies these differentiating CO_2 initiatives and the focus of some carriers on partnering with environmentally based organizations and NGOs.

Larger carriers recognize that the vast majority of the CO_2 from transportation is from fuel and, therefore, are focusing their efforts in this area. There are two primary approaches. The first involves advanced fleet management, and alternative fuel options from higher concentrations of biofuels, to electric, natural gas, or hybrid vehicles. This group of carriers is well past the basics of changing out tires and aerodynamic equipment, as the next steps are more significant. The second focus is on improved utilization of equipment, buildings, and logistics centers. By improving load factors in their operations and for their customers, more freight can be moved in the same CO_2 footprint. The use of enhanced packaging design tools, pallet loading, and trailer loading, internally and externally, CO_2 per shipment and per ton mile can be reduced. For

Table 6.1 Actionable CO_2 reduction practices

Common CO_2 initiatives

Facilities
- Electricity
  - Low-energy lighting, motion sensors, work hours, thermostats, energy star appliances

- Recycling
  - Refuse, pallets, lighting, metal, oil, plastic, paper, cardboard

- Resources
  - Auto towel dispensers, auto soap dispensers

- Water
  - Waterless toilets, auto flush toilets, auto faucets

Fleet
- Drivers
  - Shifting, idling, idle shutoffs, EZ pass, speed policies, minimize out-of-route miles

- Equipment
  - Speed governors, MPG monitors, recap tires, low-profile tires, bio diesel, air fairings, side fairings, routine maintenance, tire-pressure policies, aerodynamic mud flaps, trailer skirting, low idle RPM

Proactive/strategic CO_2 initiatives

Facilities
- Electricity
  - Solar panels, wind turbines, geothermal

- Recycling
  - Ink cartridges, computers, refrigerant, fluorescents, LEDs fleet

- Drivers
  - GPS routings, dispatch tools, poster programs

- Equipment
  - Electric delivery vehicles, natural gas vehicles, hybrid vehicles, intermodal, synthetic oil, synthetic lubes, fuel-sensing systems, LED lights, aluminum fuel tanks, efficient starters—brakes—engines, low drag paint, plural component paint spraying, green cleaning, aggressive equipment replacement plan, center fuse brake drums, wide-based tires, minimize tractor-trailer gap, single drive axle, trailer boattail, automated tire inflation, stationary fifth wheel

Operations
- Efficiency
  - Cube utilization tools, routing tools, physical distribution modeling, used pallet and corrugated dunnage, waste-reduction wash system, solvent cleaner/reuse system, propane fork truck conversion

- Administration
  - EDI/Web, paperless systems, driver document scanning, third-party CO_2 reduction verification

those customers actively looking to reduce their Scope 3 CO_2 footprint, this proactive approach is effective while also understanding sustainable value maximization.

Other differentiating strategies found in the sustainability initiatives of the larger carrier groups involve the advanced practices of carbon offsets and carbon trading. For example, UPS offers a carbon-neutral shipping option by which a freight premium is directed to one of the four global environmental projects that will reduce carbon as much or more than that generated by the shipment. Although eliminating CO_2 is preferred to offsetting it, the continued dependence on fossil fuels for transportation in the foreseeable future requires other alternatives to neutralize the effect of transport CO_2. One missing practice for a long-term sustainable relationship with nearly all LTL carriers is a formal strategic position on sustainability. While some LTL carriers such as PITT OHIO have a web page and literature about their "green" initiatives, a review of other service provider's strategic plans and value statements uncovers an absence of a formal statement of strategic sustainability improvement as a corporate goal. Often any mention of sustainability programs by LTL providers is buried in web pages that require searches to locate, while the larger, more proactive carriers prominently display their sustainable programs, affiliations, performance metrics, and their strategic commitment to sustainability.

The most visible difference between LTL sustainability programs and the large national LTL, TL, and multimode carriers is the existence of, or lack of an annual sustainability report. While these reports, in some cases, are very extensive (FedEx 47 pages and UPS 107 pages), the size is not as important as making an open declaration of past sustainable accomplishments and future goals. Annual sustainability reports provide current and prospective customers with transparency into the organization's sustainability strategies and establish a level of accountability, providing customers an assurance that sustainability is a critical part of the carrier's future. By identifying both accomplishments and future plans, customers can understand a compelling story of the value placed on sustainability by the carrier, and how well the carrier's goals align with their own. For those shippers that are held accountable by offshore

Table 6.2 Best-in-class sustainability differentiating initiatives

Customer focus	<ul><li>Carbon Exchanges<ul><li>The Carbon Neutral Company</li><li>Carbon Fund</li></ul></li><li>Carbon Offsets<ul><li>Gold Standard</li><li>Voluntary Carbon Standards (VCS)</li><li>Climate Action Reserve (CAR)</li><li>EU Allowance</li><li>Certified Emissions Reduction</li><li>ATA Sustainability Task Force</li><li>American Transportation Research Institute (ATRI)</li></ul></li><li>Promote Green Initiatives<ul><li>Advanced fleet management</li><li>AI and machine learning</li><li>Logistics centers utilizing solar and renewable energy technologies</li><li>Materiality</li><li>President's message</li><li>Strategic plans</li><li>Sustainability Report</li><li>CO_2 goals (percentage reduction by given year)</li><li>Circular economy</li></ul></li><li>Sustainability Indeces<ul><li>Carbon Disclosure Project</li><li>Dow Jones</li><li>Global Reporting Initiative (GRI)</li></ul></li></ul>
<ul><li>Package design support</li><li>Sustainable packaging</li><li>Shipment scheduling</li><li>Carbon neutral options</li><li>Carbon calculators</li><li>Stakeholder engagement and collaboration</li></ul>*Environmental key performance indicators*<ul><li>CO_2 per ship unit</li><li>CO_2 per $ sales</li><li>Decarbonizing</li><li>Water (gallons) per unit</li><li>Alternative fuels</li><li>Renewable energy</li><li>Environmental and sustainability affiliates<ul><li>Forest ethics</li><li>Dogwood alliance</li><li>BSR</li><li>SGS in the United States</li><li>Global Resource Initiative</li><li>GreenWay</li><li>US Green Building Council and LEED</li><li>Net-zero energy</li><li>Trees for the Future</li><li>International Green Energy Council</li><li>Green Geeks</li></ul></li></ul>	

parent companies for improving their carbon footprint, alignment with strategically committed sustainable carriers is a positive step toward meeting parent company goals and the UN SDGs.

The LTL Carrier Context Summary

Our research suggests that any firm integrating sustainability should provide a compelling story to customers regarding the benefits of their previous carbon emission improvements and the development of a program for continued improvement. Industry trends point to the need for more visibility and transparency in reporting carbon reduction efforts, opportunities for providing lower carbon services, and developing sustainability reports to position any firm relative to others in its industry.

Some firms such as PITT OHIO are already positioned to expand their competitive lead over LTL carriers due to proactive efforts toward environmental sustainability. By going beyond the basic steps of energy and CO_2 reduction to full carbon footprint accounting and customer-specific CO_2 allocation, some will outperform other LTL carriers and can offer sustainability conscious customers verifiable data on their Scope 3 supply chain footprints.

As a result of measurement and reporting, transparent, publicly traded firms can be included in rankings such as Newsweek's Greenest Companies and within socially responsible investing (SRI) indexes such as the Dow Jones Sustainability Index, MSCI, or FTSE 4 Good. The future reality of supply chain management is an integrated approach where supply chain professionals will leverage visibility within a supply chain to impact financial performance while simultaneously measuring, managing, and reporting natural AND social capital as enablers of transparency.

Summary

In this chapter, we have looked at performance and the factors contributing to more, not less comprehension of your processes and those of your suppliers. We need to start thinking about second- and third-tier suppliers, negative externalities, and how technology is enabling more systems integration. We have introduced programs and guidelines to help you measure and manage processes in new ways. These approaches from the SmartWay, SCOR, GRI, and CDP all indicate that environmental and social performance measurement is here to stay as a more holistic view of opportunities and supply chain relationships. What appears to be a revolution to many has become an evolution to some. After reviewing applicable models, protocols, and initiatives, a deep dive into the carrier and LTL industry demonstrates the ability to understand an organization's carbon footprint assessment. There is always room for improvement as supply chains integrate sustainability and this metric evolution to innovate, reduce waste, and maximize sustainable value.

Applied Learning: Action Items (AIs)—Steps You Can Take to Apply the Learning From This Chapter

AI: Are you or your suppliers participants in the SmartWay program?

AI: Where in the Green SCOR are there opportunities to better understand your own processes?

AI: Search for GRI reports from other firms in your industry? What do you find?

AI: Evaluate your firm's practices to assess energy consumption and associated emissions. Do you have more Scope 1, 2, or 3 GHG emissions?

AI: Review the CDP's supply chain program. What can you and your suppliers learn from this to help achieve climate resilience?

Further Readings

Global Reporting Initiative, www.globalreporting.org/Pages/default.aspx.

Carbon Disclosure Project Supply Chain Program, www.cdp.net/en/supply-chain.

GHG Protocol Calculation Tools, www.ghgprotocol.org/calculation-tools.

Environmental Protection Agency's SmartWay Program, www.epa.gov/smartway.

Sustainable Accounting Standards Board (SASB) Materiality Maps across industry sectors, https://sasb.ifrs.org/standards/materiality-map/.

DuJon, V., J. Dillard, and E. M. Brennan. *Social Sustainability: A Multi Level Approach to Social Inclusion,* NY, New York: Rout-ledge, 2013.

Sheffi, Y. *The New (Ab) normal: Reshaping Business Supply Chains Strategy Beyond COVID-19.* MIT CLM Media, 2020.

PART 3

The Key Activities of a Strategic Sustainable Supply Chain

CHAPTER 7

Standards in Support of S³CM

A sustainable environment requires increased productivity; productivity comes about by innovation; innovation is the result of investment; and investment is only possible when a reasonable return is expected. The efficient use of money is more assured when there are known standards in which to operate.

—Robert Lane, CEO Deere & Company

Living in a World of Standards

- With over 23,000 GRI reports recorded in their database, sustainability reporting continues to grow. The GRI produces a comprehensive sustainability reporting framework that is widely used around the world to enable greater organizational transparency. The framework, including the reporting guidelines, sets out the principles and indicators that organizations can use to measure and report their material financial, environmental, and social performance. GRI is committed to continuously improving the guidelines, which are freely available to the public. www.globalreporting.org/

- The U.S. SEC rules requiring companies to assess and report on their sourcing and chain of custody of certain "conflict minerals" as mandated by the Dodd–Frank Wall Street Reform and Consumer Protection Act.[*] These minerals—tin, tungsten, and gold—are typically mined illegally and in breach of human

---

[*]See U.S. Securities and Exchange Commission; at www.sec.gov/opa/Article/2012-2012-163htm---related-materials.html.

rights in the Democratic Republic of Congo and surrounding countries, and their sales are used to fund ongoing civil war. This is the SEC's venture into reporting rules on social and environmental issues; earlier it adopted guidance on board diversity.

- More recently, the SEC has adopted guidance on reporting climate change impacts of firms and GHG emissions. In 2024, the U.S. SEC adopted new rules that require public companies to disclose detailed information about climate change in their SEC filings. The rules apply to all types of registrants, including domestic registrants and foreign private issuers (FPIs). The information must be disclosed in annual reports, registration statements, and notes to audited financial statements.[1]

- Underwriters Laboratories, well known for establishing product safety standards and certification processes, issued a sustainability standard for manufacturing organizations, a certifiable standard framed around five topics: governance for sustainability, environment, workforce, customers and suppliers, and community engagement and human rights.[†]

- Clorox launched a Green Works product line. This line consists of all-purpose cleaners, cleaning wipes, glass cleaners, toilet bowl cleaners, dishwashing liquids, and laundry detergents. With over 5,000 new products being introduced every year that claimed to be green or natural, the challenge facing Clorox was how to convince the marketplace that their products were green. To overcome this challenge, Clorox partnered first with the Sierra Club to review the formula and to earn third-party certification. Next, it worked through the EPA's Design for the Environment (DfE) program. Finally, it obtained the Natural Products Association Natural Home Care standard. The reason that Clorox focused on these standards was to secure trust from its customer base.

In all of these examples, we see increased reporting and sustainability initiatives being successfully pursued by companies with direct

---

[†]Underwriters Laboratory and GreenBiz Group.

implications for supply chains and their management. Yet, we also see some of the challenges encountered as these firms pursue more strategic sustainability practices.

For some, it was developing a system for sustainability; for others it involves securing the trust of target customers and in demonstrating a commitment to sustainability. In each of these instances, the firms involved turned to sustainability standards for the solution. Standards, while important, are only one of the many tools that are available to managers who want to make their supply chains sustainable.

Objectives

1. Review the sources and types of standards.
2. Highlight prominent standards supporting sustainability initiatives.
3. Understand how to apply these standards to enable the integration of strategic sustainability into organizations and supply chains.

Standards—Providing Guidance and Structure

A standard is a set of rules, guidelines, or characteristics for activities or systems. Typically set down in a formal document and established by a committee through consensus, the standard often provides metrics for assessing performance and offers a means for certification (formal recognition that the organization has satisfied certain minimum sets of requirements prescribed by the standard). In the case of certification, the certification process is often done in one of two ways: (a) through self-reporting by the firm; and (b) through a formal certification process carried out by an impartial third party. The latter is often viewed as being more credible in the marketplace.

Standards are a common feature in today's business environment. In the United States today, there are over 100,000 standards at work. These standards come in many forms:

- *Product-based* standards (e.g., qualified products must deliver the features and performance demanded by consumers, in addition to increased energy efficiency).
- *Performance-based* standards (e.g., level of GHG emissions, grown using Fair Trade practices).
- *Management system* standards (e.g., ISO 14001 and the environmental management system).
- *Personnel certification* standards (e.g., a person who understands production and inventory management procedures because they are Certified in Production and Inventory Management (CPIM) —a professional certification standard developed and administered by the Association for Operations Management [APICS]).
- *Construction standards for buildings* (e.g., Leadership in Energy and Environmental Design or LEED, Living Buildings from the International Living Future Institute, and WELL Buildings).

Standards can come from several different sources, the most important of which are the following:

- *Governmental agencies* (e.g., the United States Department of Agriculture with its Organic Standards Program, and EPA's Energy Star Program)
- *NGOs* (e.g., ISO, headquartered in Geneva, Switzerland, CDP, SASB, or the GRI).
- *Professional societies* (e.g., APICS with its CPIM certification program)
- *Consultants/Consulting organizations* (e.g., the C2C design standard developed by the McDonough Braungart Design Chemistry [MBDC] consultants)
- *Individual Organizations/Firms.* In some cases, such as with Abhold International's Utz Certified or Starbuck's and its C.A.F.E. program or Nespresso's AAA ecolaboration program, an individual company with sufficient market presence or power can successfully introduce a standard

Standards also have different levels of "intensity":

- *Mandatory*: You must conform to the standard or you are not allowed to sell your product or compete. Failure to be certified can also result in being fined or otherwise punished.
- *Quasimandatory*: While certification is not legally required, it is so strongly encouraged that it is viewed as almost being mandatory. A good example is that of ISO 9000 (the quality process standard). Increasingly, to compete in many industries such as the auto or aerospace, or markets, you must first be ISO 9000 certified.
- *Voluntary*: This is the least intense of the standards. Certification is requested but not necessary. An example of this type of standard is the C2C design standard. Often, these standards, while driven by important goals and considerations, are voluntary because they have not achieved a sufficiently high level of acceptance/use to become viewed as quasimandatory. Within some industries, for example, office furniture, Steelcase has been able to differentiate its products with claims of having the most C2C certified products. This is particularly important when competing against Herman Miller—a company with a history of environmentally responsible design and awards.

Without a standard, there is no logical basis for making a decision or taking actions.

—Joseph M. Juran

Types of Standards

Generally, standards can derive from either an absolute goal or a relative outcome. An *absolute standard* is based on some performance goal that is independent of the process being studied or a process that is theoretically capable of being a "best practice." For example, the EPA mandates that certain manufacturing processes only allow a maximum amount of pollution emissions per day. This mandate forms an absolute standard against which performance is compared. An example of the second type of absolute standard is given by a time and motion study, which calculates the absolute minimum time required to perform a given set of tasks.

Relative standards derive from reference points given by the past performance of the process or given by the performance of other similar processes. In general, there are three major types of relative standards: (a) internal standards, (b) group standards, and (c) benchmarks.

An *internal relative standard* is defined by the past performance of the person or process being measured. The current performance is compared with the past performance, and the difference is noted. For example, a manufacturing plant's GHG emissions (a measure of waste) for a given month could be compared with its emissions for the same month a year earlier. Such a standard is easy to implement and understand; its goals and intentions are unambiguous. Yet, there are potential problems with this approach. First, it is often difficult to determine if differences in performance over time are due to changes within the process or due to external factors outside the control of managers. For example, if our plant produced fewer emissions this year than last year at the same time, is it because we are more efficient, or are there other causes, such as a reduced market share?

A *group relative standard* is based on the performance of other groups or processes that perform similar tasks to those we are interested in measuring. For example, we might compare energy conservation across different manufacturing plants within our plant network, or within our industry. We can also assess our supply base on dimensions of quality, environmental management systems, or human rights infractions. One use of this type of standard is to identify the best performer and to compare everyone else to this best performer. This approach deals with the limitations of internal relative standards, yet it has two shortcomings. The first is the possibility that even the best performer in the comparison group is doing a poor job. The second and more troubling concern is determining what constitutes a comparable group. Few processes, people, or groups are completely comparable—differences exist. It is up to you, and/or the manager of a metric to attempt to identify and maintain a suitable group of comparable processes for comparison, recognizing that the group membership may change over time.

The ultimate form of the relative standard is the *benchmark,* defined as a standard of performance representing the best in a given class of performers. In business, a benchmark is a widely accepted standard that denotes above average to "world-class" performance. Generally, there are three levels of benchmarks—best in firm (BIF), best in industry (BII), and best in class (BIC). The expected level of performance increases as we move from BIF to BIC benchmarks.

Establishing and using benchmarks can be costly. Consequently, benchmarking is usually reserved for strategically important processes. To appreciate the importance of benchmarking, consider the following story. A computer manufacturer operates its own division for supporting field service (repairs to computers). Inventory accuracy is important in this activity to ensure that needed parts are in stock to support field service personnel. After several years of hard work, this manufacturer had improved its inventory accuracy from about 75 percent to about 95 percent. Everyone in the division was proud, and others in the company were impressed, until at a conference one of the division managers learned that typical inventory accuracy levels in the pharmaceutical industry were 99 percent. Soon, the division managers sent a team to visit a drug company, where they found that inventory accuracy was actually 99.99 percent. More importantly, the team learned many valuable lessons regarding how the drug company had achieved this high level of performance.

From this example, we can see that a benchmark is a standard of performance that represents the best or highest levels. How we define the "best" is a result of how we define the boundaries of the context in which we will search for benchmarks: within the firm, within the industry, or within all "comparable" operations. A question to ask is, "can we get to zero?," that is, zero waste, zero errors, zero energy, zero emissions, or carbon neutrality, and backcast from this to look at what is feasible as BIF or BIC.

As another example of BIC benchmarking, consider that when a medical products manufacturer wanted to benchmark the integration of sustainability into the new product development process, they chose DuPont, a chemical company. Why a science-based chemical company? DuPont has created a sustainability index[2] that assesses products over 11 different criteria; these include: climate change (measured in GHG emissions generated throughout the life cycle of the product), energy use, pollution (both air and water created during product use), material use (and recycled content), waste disposal, ecosystems and biodiversity, water consumption, toxicological risk, use of nondepletable resources, and cradle-to-gate environmental footprint. DuPont's ability to integrate dimensions of sustainability into a phased gate approach was known across industries. This process was "comparable" to the medical product's new development requirements.

Standards: Pros and Cons

In most cases, becoming or requiring certification is a time-consuming and often expensive process. It requires top management support; a champion from within the company to make a business case to both the firm's top management and to the rank and file that certification is both necessary and beneficial. It also entails marketing costs to explain the standards and its benefits/implications to key customers and/or stakeholders. Finally, it takes time to become certified—to learn about the standard; to do an initial audit with the goal of identifying those areas where the firm needs to do more work; to develop and implement a corrective action plan to address the issues uncovered in the audit; and, to then undergo final certification. Given the time and resources required, this raises a simple but important question—why become certified?

Standards are attractive because they offer management and stakeholders several advantages:

Standards are often based on codified "best practices." Ultimately, a standard reflects the "best practices" that have been found to work in other organizations. That is, when a standard such as ISO 14001 is created, the committee responsible for creating it reviews all of the practices associated with effective/successful examples. These practices are then reviewed, and the most important practices identified. These form the foundation on which the standard is built. The advantage of this approach is that we are drawing on practices that we know are important and that we know work (and work well). This process simplifies life for the organization being certified (since they do not have to research and identify these practices).

Standards provide a template for organizations interested in developing new systems. A template can be regarded as a guide to help organizations implement a new system or activity. This guide takes two forms. First, there is a process guide. This guide tells the organizations what activities they must implement and in what order. The second is a content guide. That is, the standard tells the organization what activities must be present if the organization wants to implement a certain system. For example, if you are interested in having an environmental management system, ISO 14001 will identify the minimum set of components that you must have for that system.

Standards have marketing value. As we saw in the case of Clorox (described in the opening vignettes), the adoption of standards can have strong marketing value. The reason—the standards convey credibility. For certain markets and customers, knowing that the firms they are working with are certified in certain standards has a real value—a value that can be manifested in one of two ways. First, the certified firms are given preference when it comes to purchases. Second, the buyers are willing to pay a price premium for their products.

Standards provide strong signals regarding the organization's intents. Closely associated with the preceding issue is the notion of signaling. Signaling is an approach whereby our actions are viewed as signals we send to others. When we tell the market that we are actively pursuing a certain standard, we can be viewed as effectively sending the following signals: (a) the activity or system underlying the standard is important to our firm; (b) we are committed to this activity or system; and (c) we are willing to spend the time and resources to attain the necessary certification. In many cases, these are strong signals.

Standards are often supported by other organizations. Implementing a new standard is a major undertaking (as previously noted). What simplifies this process is that standards are often supported by an infrastructure consisting of consultants, educators, professional societies, and educational/training material. The consultants provide specific assistance in terms of what the standards mean, how the organization can implement them, whether the organization is ready, and what it must do to be ready. Similarly, educators help collect and consolidate material about standards, thus helping to improve awareness and learning about them. Professional societies such as APICS , Institute for Supply Management (ISM) , Supply Chain Council (SCC), Council for Supply Chain Management Professionals (CSCMP), the International Society of Sustainability Professionals (ISSP), and the Alliance for Strategic Sustainable Development (ASSD) (to name a few) provide support in many ways to organizations interested in exploring and implementing specific standards and tools. These organizations provide information. Through meetings (either at the national/international level or the more local chapter level), they provide venues where the organizations can meet and talk with others who have gone through the process or who are currently going through the process of implementing the new standard. The societies also help keep organizations up to date on changes in the standards or their implementation. Finally, the standards are often accompanied by educational material in the form of books (available either online or through actual books sold by outlets such as Amazon), magazine articles, and online postings. Again, this provides needed information and guidance to the organizations so that they know they are not alone in this effort.

Standards are often accompanied by metrics. As previously pointed out in Chapter 5, a metric consists of three interrelated elements: a measure, a standard, and a consequence. What this means to the organizations pursuing the standard is that they now know *operationally* how the standard and the performance associated with the standard is measured. They also know what the minimum level of acceptable performance is, so that they can evaluate their own levels of performance. Finally, these metrics, since they are common, enable firms to compare their performance levels with those reported by others.

Standards simplify evaluation and assessment. This last advantage is most relevant when dealing with supply chains. With supply chains, we have many different firms involved as suppliers. Without standards, we would have to individually assess each firm, its systems, and its performance. This is a very time-consuming and resource-intensive effort. Standards greatly simplify this process. To assess the supply chain partners, we simply determine whether or not they have attained the necessary certification. If they have, then we have one strong indication that they are acceptable.

Against these advantages, you have to recognize the downsides created by standards:

Standards often lag behind leading edge practices. It takes time for a practice to be recognized as "best." That is, the practice must be first implemented, and its impact identified. Then, the practice must become known outside of the firm that first developed it. Next, the practice must show that it can persistently contribute to improved results. Then, it can become recognized as a best practice. What this means is that the practices that make up the basis of the standards may not reflect what is currently considered an innovative practice—there is always a lag.

Standards are not enough by themselves. Standards are often built around practices. These practices are generic because they are intended to be applied to the largest number of organizations. Yet, for these practices to be truly effective, two conditions must be first met. First, they must fit within the organization, its culture, and its past. If they don't fit, the practices will not be embraced and implemented. Second, they have to be extended. The practices have to be taken, used, and built upon to create new forms of value. It is the ability to fit and extend that often differentiates the successful firms with the implementation and usage of standards from those that simply do enough to be considered certified.

Being certified does not necessarily mean that the firm really embraces the systems or the activities. This concern follows from the preceding point. Just because an organization is certified does not necessarily mean that the firm has achieved the desired outcomes. It is one thing to do enough to become certified in any of the sustainability standards (e.g., ISO 14001). To be certified, all that is often required is for the firm to hire a consultant who can help the firm walk through the process and meet the certification requirements. It is quite another thing to embrace sustainability and rebuild systems around standards. Certification is a long-term undertaking that requires an understanding of sustainability and its goals, top management, and significant investments of time and resources. Consequently, taking a limited view of certification and sustainability often makes sense. When a firm attains certification in a specific standard, such as ISO 14001, this should not mean that the firm has a system that is built around sustainability. Rather, it should be viewed as the firm being certified—nothing more and nothing less.

Standards may not be attractive to firms that have achieved the same outcomes by pursuing different approaches. Standards often identify one way or path of achieving a specific outcome or implementing a specific system. Other approaches are as effective in the end. The problem is that to be certified, some firms may see an additional cost— that of changing their existing systems simply to meet the certification requirements. The resulting benefits may not be viewed as sufficient to offset the costs. The authors encountered such a situation when they studied ISO 14001. They encountered a firm that had developed a highly effective system for sustainability. Initially, when they became aware of ISO 14001, management thought it might be useful to become one of the first American firms to achieve this certification. However, when they looked at the requirements for ISO 14001 certification, and compared these requirements with the existing system, management came to the conclusion that they would have to invest extensively to meet the certification requirements. These investments were not seen as having any impact on the firm's ability to improve its sustainability perform-ance. As one manager told the authors, "this is an investment simply in paper and administration." Consequently, the firm decided NOT to pursue ISO 14001 certification. *Standards can discourage risk-taking.* Finally, standards identify desired objectives and appropriate approaches. As long as the firm pursues these objectives using approved approaches, it can expect to avoid problems. However, should the firm identify a new and potentially more attractive way of achieving these same objectives, then the firm assumes the costs of demonstrating that this cost is better. Consequently, firms may be discouraged from pursuing new and different approaches.

As can be seen from this discussion, standards are important. Yet, they are imperfect indicators of sustainability. Consequently, they should be leveraged with great care and alignment with your business model, that is, value proposition, capabilities, and key customers (Chapter 2). Next, we want to highlight some of the well-known sustainability standards. This list is not all-inclusive, but instead a brief review and opportunity to get started in finding more information on standards that may be directly applied to your own organization.

Sustainability Standards

To this point, we have discussed the need for standards; and identified some different standards and certifications. In this section, we turn our attention to identifying the sustainability standards out there. The reality is that the number of standards related to sustainability is growing every day. Some of the more commonly cited sustainability standards are presented in Table 7.1. As can be seen from this table, these standards cover a wide range of sustainability-related issues.

Standards and Sustainability—Understanding the Challenges

Standards play a potentially important role in S³CM in that they provide the management of the focal firm with a potentially effective means of communicating the need for sustainability within the supply chain. In Chapter 1, we pointed out that sustainability was an example of a SCSI. That is, for the focal firm to succeed with sustainability, it must promote sustainability not only within the firm but also within the supply chain. As previously discussed, this means that sustainability must be embraced at every stage of the extended supply chain—at the first tier, second tier, third tier, and so on. Yet, this presents a problem for the focal firm—how to ensure that the importance of sustainability to the suppliers of this extended supply chain and how to assess the extent of compliance. This challenge is amplified by the fact that most

Table 7.1 Examples of sustainability standards/initiatives

Program/initiative	Source	Summary
Social Standards		
Accountability, Assurance and Stakeholder Engagement: AA1000 standards www.accountability.org/	Accountability	These standards help organizations address issues affecting governance, business models, and organizational strategy, as well as provide operational guidance on sustainability assurance and stakeholder engagement. The AA1000 standards are designed for the integrated thinking required by the low-carbon and green economy, and support integrated reporting and assurance.
SA8000 www.sa-intl.org/	Social Accountability International (SAI)	This is a voluntary, universal standard for companies interested in auditing and certifying social performance. It is one of the world's first auditable social certification standards for decent workplaces, across all industrial sectors. It is based on conventions of the International Labor Organization, United Nations, and national laws. The SA8000 standard spans industry and corporate codes to create a common language for measuring social compliance.
Fair Trade www.fairtradeusa.org/, www.fairtrade.net/	Fair Trade USA Fair Trade International	Initially developed in the 1940s when a few small North American and European organizations reached out to help poor communities and supply chains sell their products to well-off markets. Today, fair trade is a global effort aimed at helping poor countries and areas by relieving exploitation and promoting environmental, economic, and social sustainability. Currently, Fair Trade USA, formerly a licensing agency for the Fair Trade International label, has broken from the system and is creating its own labeling scheme.
Financial Reporting www.ifrs.org/	International Financial Reporting	The IFRS develops high-quality, understandable, enforceable, and globally accepted accounting and sustainability disclosure standards influencing strategic sustainable supply chain management.

(Continued)

Table 7.1 *(Continued)*

Program/initiative	Source	Summary
	Standards Foundation (IFRS)	
Human Rights www.ohchr.org/EN/HRBodies/HRC/Pages/HRCIndex.aspx	United Nations Human Rights Council	The Guiding Principles for Business and Human Rights are an actionable set of processes and guidelines for global business designed to provide a global standard for preventing and addressing the risk of adverse impacts on human rights linked to business activity.
International Disclosure https://www.ifrs.org/groups/international-sustainability-standards-board/	International Sustainability Standards Board (ISSB)	The ISSB develops global sustainability disclosure standards integrating ESG metrics, climate-related financial disclosure, stakeholder engagement, helping to understand risk management, and creating long-term value.
Intergovernmental Panel on Climate Change https://www.ipcc.ch/report/ar6/wg3/chapter/chapter-11/	IPCC	Established in 1988, the work of the IPCC influences supply chain management through its assessment reporting, the ability of scientific evidence leading to regulatory changes, risk management, and sustainability goals for companies' investor and consumer expectations, along with innovation and adaptation. Examples of its influence can be found in carbon footprint reductions, resource efficiency, and circular economy practices.
Organic Certification www.usda.gov/wps/portal/usda/usdhome	USDA	The USDA National Organic Program regulates the standards of any farm or organization that seeks to sell an agricultural product as organically produced. The National Organic Program and the Organic Foods Production Act are intended to assure consumers that the organic foods they purchase are produced, processed, and certified to be consistent with national organic standards.

(Continued)

Table 7.1 (Continued)

Program/initiative	Source	Summary
Rainforest Alliance http://www.rainfores-talliance.org	Rainforest Alliance	Created in the late 1980s from a social movement, the Rainforest Alliance is committed to conserving biodiversity and ensuring sustainable livelihoods (especially for those living in rainforest areas). One key feature of the standard and the associated certification process is the requirement for a detailed plan for the development of a sustainable farm management system to protect and encourage wildlife conservation.
Responsible Care www.responsiblecare.org	Chemical Industry	Responsible Care is a voluntary initiative of the global chemical industry to safely handle products from inception in the research laboratory, through manufacture and distribution, to ultimate reuse, recycle, and disposal, and to involve the public in decision-making processes.
Sustainable Development Goals (SDGs) https://sustainabledevelopment.un.org/sdgs	United Nations	The UN SDGs are a plan of action for people, planet, and prosperity. It seeks to strengthen universal peace and freedom, eradicate poverty, heal and secure the planet, while tackling the greatest global challenges of our times. There are 17 goals and 169 targets. All countries and all stakeholders, acting in collaborative partnership, will implement this plan.
Sustainable Forest Products https://us.fsc.org/	Forest Stewardship Council (FSC)	FSC is an organization protecting forests for future generations while setting standards under which forests and company's products are certified. The organization provides independent labeling and certification of products.
UTZ Certified www.utzcertified.org	UTZ Certified	This is a label and program for sustainable farming of agricultural products that was launched as a separate initiative in 2002. It currently claims to be the largest program for coffee in the world. Known formerly as Utz Kapeh (Mayan for "good coffee"), this program was first launched by the Dutch coffee roaster Ahold Coffee Company in 1997. This program aims

(Continued)

Table 7.1 (Continued)

Program/initiative	Source	Summary
		to create an open and transparent marketplace for socially and environmentally responsible agricultural products. Utz Certified is consistent with this book's view of sustainability since the 2009 Code of Conduct version focuses on three categories of performance: (1) good agricultural and business practices; (2) social criteria; and (3) environmental criteria.
UL880 www.ul.com/ global/eng/pages/offerings/businesses/environment/ services/sq/enterprisestandards/UL880/index.jsp	Underwriters Laboratory and GreenBiz Group	UL Environment collaborated with GreenBiz Group, a leader in corporate sustainability media, corporate sustainability leadership and reporting, to develop UL 880: Sustainability for Manufacturing Organizations that includes governance, the environment, workforce, customers and suppliers, along with community engagement and human rights.
Environmental Standards		
Carbon Disclosure www.cdproject.net	CDP	An independent not-for-profit organization working to drive down GHG emissions and sustainable water use by businesses and cities. Based on the premise that the first step in managing GHG emissions and sustainable water usage is that of measurement. CDP holds the world's largest collection of self-reported climate change data.
Carbon Offsets www.co2offsetresearch.org/policy/VoluntaryStd.html	American Carbon Registry Social Carbon Climate Action Reserve. The Clean Development Mechanism Gold	There are over a dozen standards (with only six listed here) to verify the legitimacy of an offset provider by numerous combinations of metrics. An inclusive, complete, and credible carbon offset standard should include the following criteria: accounting standards; monitoring, verification, and certification standards; and registration and enforcement systems.[3] The motivation for reporting GHG emissions and purchasing offsets includes corporate public relations and corporate social responsibility, a desire to go beyond what

(Continued)

Table 7.1 (Continued)

Program/initiative	Source	Summary
	Standard Verified Carbon Standard	is mandated in terms of emission reductions, and to prepare for expected compliance action, for example, the introduction of a cap-and-trade system.
Conflict Minerals www.sec.gov/news/press/ 2012/2012-163.htm	Organization for Economic Cooperation and Development (OECD) Securities and Exchange Commission	The OECD published the guidance on conflict minerals supply chain traceability. This guidance is gaining momentum as "the" standard within U.S. policy. However, an analysis of the standard in comparison to existing U.S. auditing standards under SEC highlighted a number of significant inconsistencies and conflict with relevant U.S. standards. Companies subject to the U.S. law who implement the OECD Guidance without regard for the SEC auditing standards may face legal-compliance risks.
Cradle-to-Cradle Standard www.mbdc.com/c2c/	McDonough Braungart Design Chemistry	A set of standards intended to ensure that products are designed to make use of renewable resources and that the resulting products can be easily disassembled and the outputs converted back into inputs for future production (rather than being returned to the ground).
Electronic Product Environmental Assessment Tool (EPEAT) www.epeat.net	Green Electronics Council	A method for evaluating the environmental impact of computers and other electronic equipment. A seal to certify that electronic products are recyclable and designed to maximize energy efficiency and minimize environmental harm. EPEAT rating is becoming a requirement for purchases placed by the U.S. government, state and city governments (e.g., San Francisco).
Energy Star www.energystar.gov/	EPA in partnership with the	Helping save money and protect the environment through the use of energy-efficient products and practices. This is more than just a label on a product as the EPA also provides an innovative energy performance rating system, which businesses have already used for more

(Continued)

Table 7.1 (Continued)

Program/initiative	Source	Summary
	Department of Energy	than 200,000 buildings across the country. EPA also recognizes top-performing buildings with the ENERGY STAR program.
Greenhouse Gas Reduction www.theclimateregistry.org/	The Climate Registry	This nonprofit organization provides information to reduce GHG emissions. The Climate Registry establishes consistent, transparent standards throughout North America for businesses and governments to calculate, verify, and publicly report their carbon footprints in a single, unified registry.
Greenhouse Gas Reporting Program www.epa.gov/ghgreporting/	EPA (USA)	Implemented in 2008, requires the mandatory reporting of GHGs of American firms. Comprehensive GHG data reported directly to EPA from across the country are now easily accessible to the public through EPA's GHG Reporting Program (GHGRP).
Greenhouse Gas Protocol www.ghgprotocol.org/	World Resources Institute World Business Council for Sustainable Development	The most widely used international accounting tool for government and business leaders to understand, quantify, and manage GHG emissions. They have worked with businesses, governments, and environmental groups around the world to build a new generation of credible and effective programs for tackling climate change. It provides the accounting framework for nearly every GHG standard and program in the world—from the ISO to The Climate Registry—as well as hundreds of GHG inventories prepared by individual companies.
Reporting www.globalreporting.org/	Global Reporting Initiative	An international, independent organization that helps businesses, governments, and other organizations understand and communicate the impact of business on critical sustainability issues such as climate change, human rights, corruption, and many others. With thousands of GRI reporting firms in over 90 countries, GRI provides the world's most widely used

(Continued)

Table 7.1 (Continued)

Program/initiative	Source	Summary
		standards on sustainability reporting and disclosure, enabling businesses, governments, civil society and citizens to make better decisions based on information that matters.
Integrated Reporting www.sasb.org/	Sustainability Accounting Standards Board (SASB)	SASB is in the business of development and dissemination of industry-specific sustainability accounting standards. The goal is to establish an understanding of material sustainability issues facing industries and create sustainability accounting standards suitable for disclosure in standard filings such as the Form 10 K and 20 F. This organization addresses the unique needs of the U.S. market, establishing standards for integrated reporting that are concise, comparable within an industry, and relevant to all publicly listed companies in the United States.
ISO 9001 Quality Management www.iso.org/iso/home/standards/management-standards/iso_9000.htm	ISO	The 9000 family of standards sets out the criteria for a quality management system (QMS) and this is the only standard in the family that can be certified (although this is not a requirement). This standard has been implemented by over one million companies and organizations in over 170 countries with total quality environmental management as a logical extension of a QMS.
ISO 14000 family of standards www.iso.org/iso/home/standards/management-standards/iso14000.htm	ISO	The family of standards gives the requirements for an environmental management and is one of more than 15,000 voluntary International Standards published by the ISO. It is primarily concerned with "environmental management." For the ISO, this means what the organization does to minimize harmful effects on the environment of its activities. It is not a product standard and does not give requirements for specific products or services; rather,

(Continued)

Table 7.1 (Continued)

Program/initiative	Source	Summary
		it provides a set of generic requirements for what the organization must do to manage the processes influencing the impact of the organization's activities on the environment.
ISO 14001 Environmental Management Systems www.iso.org/iso/home. html www.epa.gov/ems	ISO	Sets out the criteria for an environmental management system and can be certified. It does not state requirements for environmental performance, but maps out a framework that a company or organization can follow to set up an effective environmental management system. It can be used by any organization regardless of its activity or sector. Using this standard provided assurance to company management and employees as well as external stakeholders that environmental impact is being measured and improved.
ISO 14020—14,024 Environmental Labeling www.iso. org/iso/home.html	ISO	Sets out the guidelines for environmental labeling covering three types of labeling schemes: Type I is a multiattribute label developed by a third party; Type II is a single-attribute label developed by the producer; Type III is an eco-label whose awarding is based on a full LCA.
ISO 14025 Environmental Product Declarations, https://www.iso.org/standard/38131.html	ISO	Environmental Product Declarations (EPDs) are product labels that are developed by industry in accordance with the International Organization for Standardization (ISO) Standard 14,025. EPDs are also known as Type III Environmental Declarations.
ISO 14040—14,044 Life Cycle Assessment www.iso.gov/nrmrl/std/lca/lca.html http://www.epa.gov/nrmrl/std/lca/lca.html	ISO	Sets out the principles and framework for LCA including: definition of the goal and scope of the LCA, the life cycle inventory analysis (LCI) phase, the life cycle impact assessment (LCIA) phase, the life cycle interpretation phase, reporting and critical review of the LCA, limitations of the assessment, the relationship between the LCA phases, and conditions for use of value choices and optional elements.

(Continued)

Table 7.1 (Continued)

Program/initiative	Source	Summary
ISO 14064 GHG Emission Quantification and Reporting www.iso.org/iso/home.html	ISO	Sets out the principles and requirements at the organization level for quantification and reporting of GHG emissions and removals. It includes requirements for the design, development, management, reporting, and verification of an organization's GHG inventory.
ISO 20400 Sustainable Procurement	ISO	Provides guidelines for integrating sustainability into procurement processes. It encourages organizations to consider environmental, social, and economic impacts when making procurement decisions, thereby affecting supply chains.
ISO 26000 Corporate Social Responsibility www.iso.org/iso/home.html	ISO	Sets out to provide guidance rather than requirements, so it cannot be certified unlike some other ISO standards. Instead, it helps clarify what social responsibility is, helps businesses and organizations translate principles into effective actions, and shares best practices relating to social responsibility, globally. It is aimed at all types of organizations regardless of their activity, size, or location.
ISO 50001 Energy Management Systems www.iso.org/iso/home.html	ISO	Based on the management system model of continual improvement used for other standards, ISO 50001 makes it easier for organizations to integrate energy management into their overall efforts to improve quality and environmental management. This energy management standard provides a framework of requirements for organizations to: develop a policy for more efficient use of energy; fix targets and objectives to meet the policy; use data to better understand and make decisions about energy use; measure the results; review how well the policy works; and continually improve energy management.

(Continued)

Table 7.1 (Continued)

Program/initiative	Source	Summary
Living Buildings and Living Products https://living-future.org/lbc/ and https://living-future.org/lpc/	International Living Future Institute	The Living Building Challenge is the world's most rigorous proven performance standard for buildings. People from around the world use this regenerative design framework to create spaces that generate more electricity and water than they consume. The Living Product Challenge is a framework for manufacturers to create products that are healthy, inspirational and give more back to the environment than it takes to produce each unit of a product.
LEED Certification Leadership in Energy and Environmental Design www.usgbc.org/LEED/	U.S. Green Building Council (USGBC)	LEED is intended to provide building owners and operators a concise framework for identifying and implementing practical and measurable high-performance building designs, and construction, operations, and maintenance solutions. Certification can be at multiple levels; that is, silver, gold, and platinum.
United Nations Sustainable Development Goals (SDGs) https://sustainabledevelopment.un.org/sdgs	United Nations	While the SDGs are not standards, there are 17 high-level sustainability goals and 169 targets across environmental and social metrics that any organization can find relationships to as part of the 2030 Agenda for Sustainable Development connecting people, planet, prosperity, peace, and partnership.
Renewable Fuel Standard Program www.epa.gov/otaq/fuels/renewable-fuels/index.htm	EPA (USA)	Regulations designed to ensure that transportation fuel sold in the United States contains a minimum volume of renewable fuel.
Science-Based Targets initiative https://sciencebasedtargets.org/blog/new-sup	SBTi	Helps companies and financial institutions set science-based climate targets that are consistent with the latest climate science. The SBTi's Supplier Engagement Guidance,

(Continued)

Table 7.1 (*Continued*)

Program/initiative	Source	Summary
plier-engagement-guidance-unlocking-the-power-of-supply-chains-for-decarbonization		released in 2023, helps companies engage their supply chains to set targets for reducing Scope 3 emissions.
SmartWay www.epa.gov/smartway/	EPA	The SmartWay Transport Partnership is a collaboration between EPA and the freight industry. This voluntary partnership program uses strong market-based incentives to challenge companies to improve the environmental performance of their freight operations. Through their collaboration with EPA, SmartWay Transport partners improve their energy efficiency, save money, reduce GHG emissions, and improve air quality.
Sustainable Supply Chains http://supply-chain.unglobalcompact.org/	United Nations Global Compact Sustainable Supply Chains: Resources and Practices	A compendium of information for businesses seeking information about supply chain sustainability. Information designed to assist business practitioners in embedding sustainability in supply chains including initiatives, programs, codes, standards, networks, resources, and tools along with case study examples of company practices.

For more information on any standard, refer the URL hyperlink.

firms deal with supply chains where there are hundreds to thousands of suppliers and where there is diversity in the size of the suppliers, the products and/or services they provide, and their position in the supply chain (e.g., first tier versus third tier). It is not realistic nor feasible for most firms to personally visit each supplier to assess their support for sustainability. The answer to this challenge lies in sustainability standards and, as an aside, certain reporting requirements.

These standards provide an effective means of communicating requirements. That is, as a requirement of doing business with the focal firm, it is required that you, as a supplier, must either be certified (e.g., in ISO 14001) or comply with certain reporting requirements. For example, while the United States does not have a federal mandate for ESG reporting, there are regulations that require companies to disclose certain ESG information In March 2024, the U.S. SEC approved rules that compel publicly traded companies to disclose climate-related information in their annual reports and registrations statements. Consequently, a focal firm may ask their suppliers to comply with these reporting requirements.

This approach offers management certain important and attractive advantages. First, it is easy and relatively simply to implement. Second, it reduces the assessment requirements. Focal firms no longer have to visit their suppliers in order to assess the extent to which they are in compliance with the sustainability requirements of the focal firms. Current certification in the appropriate standard is deemed to be enough. It also reduces the assessment process to a simple binary decision—either you are certified, or you are not. Third, since the standards can be regarded as "codified" best practices, requiring that the suppliers be certified in these standards ensures that they are dealing with or exposed to these "best" practices. At the surface, this seems to imply that standards are critical in ensuring that supply chains at the various levels are consistent with and in support of the strategic objectives of the focal firm.

Yet, the reality is often very different!

The Realities of Standards and Sustainability

In many cases, the use of standards as a means of ensuring sustainability across the various levels creates more problems than it solves. These problems can be attributed to the following factors.

Lack of harmonizing of standards: While standards such as ISO 14001 are generic, firms often implement their own somewhat customized versions of these standards and then require their suppliers to be consistent with these "standards." If one supplier is dealing with multiple focal firms, each with their own version of the standard, the result is confusing since the supplier must deal with these various standards and the inevitable conflicts encountered. Suppliers, not the focal firms, are left with the task of addressing these conflicts.

Suppliers may not be capable of meeting these standards mandates: When dealing with standards, sustainability, and the supply chain, it is important to remember that many of the suppliers encountered will be small to medium-sized enterprises (SMEs)—that is, firms with 500 or fewer employees. It is also important to remember that these firms are NOT "small large firms"—that is, they are like large firms in terms of resources, process maturity, and capabilities—only smaller. This view assumes that SME suppliers have the same process maturity levels (i.e., they have developed and implemented formal processes for all of the major activities), similar levels of financial resources and stability, and they have access to the needed resources and expertise (in this case, as they apply to sustainability).

Unfortunately, the truth is these assumptions are often false. SME suppliers often lack financial and subject matter expertise; they do not often have the same level of process maturity. Consequently, when charged with the task of obtaining the appropriate certification or of meeting the relevant reporting requirements, they may not be able to do so. For these suppliers, sustainability becomes an additional obstacle AND cost that must be addressed and considered.

Sustainability standards often benefit the focal firm: Further compounding the difficulties raised in the preceding point is the reality of sustainability standards—while their implementation does generate certain benefits for the suppliers, the primary beneficiary is the focal firm. This creates an interesting and important economic challenge for the supplier.

To be certified in the appropriate standards, the supplier must be prepared to increase time, resources, and capital in the certification process. Yet, as previously noted, the supplier may not have access to these items. Even if they do have access, then there is a very good chance that the focal firm, not the supplier, will be the primary beneficiary. Consequently, for some suppliers, the result of these "forces" is a strong disincentive to invest in certification.

These demands may contribute to supplier "burnout": Supplier "burnout" occurs when a supplier has decided that, for whatever reason(s), it is no longer acceptable for that supplier to support that specific buying organization. Supplier burnout occurs as the result of three factors—each of which can be impacted by the demands to meet certain sustainability certification requirements or certain reporting requirements:

- *Exhaustion*: Supplier exhaustion occurs when the supplier feels that they are bombarded by a never-ending set of requirements from the focal firms. For example, the focal firm demands on a regular basis that the supplier submit certain information or data required by the focal firm.

- *Cynicism:* Cynicism describes a situation where the supplier sees the demands placed on them by the focal firm as primarily benefiting the firm, not the supplier. Whenever the focal firm presents the supplier with a new demand or initiative, the supplier automatically assumes that this request will translate into increased costs for the supplier, without much in the way of off-setting benefits.

- *Inefficacy*: Inefficacy describes a situation where the suppliers feel that the demands of the focal firm have an urgency and priority that forces the supplier to delay those activities that are critical to keeping the supplier's doors open as they direct time, money, and resources to satisfying these focal firm demands.

Often standards and reporting requirements contribute to one or more of these factors, thus increasing the probability that a supplier may decide to terminate their relationship with the focal firm. When this separation takes place, then there is the task of replacing that supplier—a task that can take anywhere from weeks to years while imposing a significant cost on the focal firm.

To illustrate this point, consider the experiences of a Fortune 50 company that purchases small quantities of high quality, precision, surgical stainless steel from a domestic (i.e., American) supplier. To the supplier, this firm is a small customer; to the firm, the supplier is critical. The firm is considering introducing a change to the supply chain (originating from one of its key customers). If the supplier decides that it is not in their best interests to comply, then it is estimated that it would take the focal firm two years to replace this supplier. This time would be consumed by identifying potential suppliers, encouraging them to become suppliers, vetting them, training and education, and finally on-boarding the new suppliers.

Being certified does not necessarily mean that the supplier is really in support of the sustainability objectives of the focal firm: Based on past research into other standards (e.g., ISO 9001 and quality), researchers have found that being certified does not necessarily mean that the organization being certified is compliant. In fact, certification can result in four outcomes:

- The supplier complies and embraces the object of the certification process.
- The supplier partially complies (the supplier picks and chooses what they want to focus).
- The supplier tells you that they are compliant when they are not (referred to as decoupling).
- The supplier does not accept the need to be certified and they quit.

The focal firm is now left with the need to ensure that the supply chain supports the sustainability objectives, while realizing that certification, while important, is not enough by itself. Then, this leads to a simple but important question—what is missing?

Addressing the Challenges of Building a Sustainable Supply Chain

To the use of standards and reporting requirements, S³CM managers must be prepared to add three more elements:

- Prioritization—identifying and focusing on the key suppliers. This element recognizes that not all suppliers are equally important.
- Being a "good" customer—understanding that relationships play an important role in any effective supply chain and that these relationships are not transaction-based alone.
- Supplier development—suppliers, especially SME suppliers, need assistance and the focal firm must be prepared to take an active role in supporting and developing these suppliers, especially in those areas relevant and critical to sustainability.

Prioritization

As has been previously pointed out, firms deal with hundreds to thousands of suppliers. At first glance, this would make the challenge of developing sustainable supply chains an enormous task. Yet, it is important to recognize that not all the suppliers are equally important. As the 19th-century Italian economist Vilfredo Pareto (1848–1923) noted, in most cases, the 20/80 rule dominates. That is, 20 percent of the suppliers account for 80 percent of the value.

In other words, managers must be prepared to identify and focus on the key suppliers. Central to this task is that of explicitly determining what constitutes a key supplier. For example, a key supplier may be one who:

- Accounts for the bulk of spent
- Is difficult to replace
- Produces an important and unique component or service.

- Is a sole sourced supplier
- Has access to critical intellectual property

This list is not meant to be comprehensive but rather illustrative.

It is important to note that in most cases commodity suppliers (i.e., suppliers of those commodities where there are multiple, readily available alternative suppliers) are not considered key suppliers.

Being a Good Customer

Once the key suppliers have been identified, the next step is to become a "good" customer. As noted by Melnyk et al. (2021),[4] being a good customer is more than simply paying on time. Drawing on a sample of over 1,300 suppliers to a single branch of the military (that they surveyed), these authors identified 21 different traits that caused a supplier to view a specific customer or buying organization as being "good"—these are summarized in Figure 7.1.

These 21 attributes were classified into four major "pillars"—see Figure 7.2. What is important to note about these four pillars is that transaction management—a central concern for most buying organizations—was deemed to be the least important by the suppliers surveyed.

There are real economic benefits to being seen by the supply chain as being a good customer. These include first access to new innovations created by the suppliers, preferred treatment by the suppliers, improved joint problem-solving, and, most important to this chapter, access to the supplier's suppliers.

To deal with an extended supply chain, with its multiple tiers of suppliers, the focal firm needs access to these lower tiers. In most cases, to get access to these lower tiers, the focal firm must work through the higher tier suppliers. That is, if you want to get access to the second tier, you need to work through the first-tier suppliers. If the first-tier supplier does not view you as a good customer, if there is no trust, then that supplier is likely to deny you access to their suppliers. By being a good customer, you develop mutual trust and respect. The suppliers trust you and are willing to give you the benefit of the doubt. If you ask to get access to their suppliers, they are more likely to do so.

ATTRIBUTE NAME	ATTRIBUTE DESCRIPTION
TRUST	Mutual trust and respect
PROFIT	Profitability of dealing with the customer
PROBLEMS	Joint problem solving
SIMPLERFP	Simple and complete Request for Quotation/Request for Proposals
TIMELYAWD	Timely awarding of contracts
CLARITY	Clarity of interactions
PREDREVNU	Predictability of revenue flow
CONFLICT	Effective conflict resolution systems
OVERALL	Overall ease of doing business
OPENNESS	Openness to suggestions and improvements from suppliers
EARLYWRN	Early warnings (regarding orders, problems, opportunities)
LTCOMMIT	Long-term commitment to suppliers
FREQCOMM	Frequency of communication (rather than only communication when there is a problem or a bid to be placed)
TRANSPART	Transparency of projects and purchases
PERMEAS	Effective, meaningful performance measures
MISSION	Clear mission and statement
CONSISTMESS	Consistency of messages/measures across levels and organizations
RISK	Risk sharing
INTEROP	Good interoperability (i.e., ability to link processes and share data).
SUPPLIERIMP	Programs for supplier improvement (in response to performance issues)
SUPPLIERDP	Supplier development programs

Figure 7.1 Customer attractiveness attributes (Melnyk et al. 2021, 44)

Supplier Development

Having prioritized the suppliers and having built a good working relationship with the key suppliers, the last step is that of supplier development. This is critical in the case of SME suppliers—suppliers that we need but that may lack the resources, process maturity, or expertise needed to support sustainability. To remedy these "weaknesses," the focal firm may have to engage in tailored supplier development. Such development may take various forms depending on the needs of the suppliers:

- Access to expertise in areas pertaining to sustainability.
- Encouragement to pursue certification through inducements such as evergreen contracts (i.e., if you become ISO 14001 certified, then as long as you maintain your certification, your contract will be more readily renewed or expanded compared to those suppliers who are not certified).

RELATIONSHIP MANAGEMENT	COMMUNICATION FLOW	SUPPLIER COMMITMENT	TRANSACTION MANAGEMENT
• Problem solving	• Performance measurement	• Supplier development	• Timely awarding of contracts
• Conflict resolution	• Consistency of message	• Long-term commitment	• Simple RFP
• Clarity of objectives	• Transparency	• Interoperability	• Predictable revenue
• Mutual trust and respect	• Frequency of communication	• Supplier development (problem driven)	• Overall ease of doing business
• Mission	• Early warning		• Profitability
• Openness			
• Risk sharing			

Figure 7.2 Being a "good" customer—the four pillars of success (Melnyk et al. 2021, 46)

- Financial support. For example, you may want to give your suppliers loans that can be used to become certified. These loans can either be low interest or forgivable (when the supplier becomes certified).
- Access to other suppliers who have gone through the certification process (so that the supplier can learn from the experience of other similar firms).
- Access to certification resources (e.g., certification templates or consultants).

With this approach, the focal firm has developed a firm foundation on which to successfully deploy standards within their supply chain.

In this chapter, we have looked at standards as a way of providing structure to measurement and management of supply chain performance. Examples of sustainability standards and initiatives show the depth and breadth of their influence on supply chain management. Next, we tried to look at and understand the challenges of working with these standards before addressing the challenges of prioritization, what it takes to be a good customer, and supplier development.

What to Do With Standards and Certifications?

As you can see, there have been numerous sustainability standards developed to address issues of social equity, environmental quality, and economic prosperity of global production and trade practices. Despite similarities in major goals and certification procedures, there are some significant differences in terms of their development, target groups of adopters, geographical diffusion, use within supply chains, and emphasis on TBL performance. Using these standards and certification properly requires that management address the following questions:

- *Why?* What is it that I am trying to achieve with the use of standards and certification? Am I interested in getting the standard because it is required for a contract or am I using the standard as a means to bring about significant change in the organization?
- *What?* What aspect of sustainability is it that I am trying to focus attention on?
- *How much?* How much time and what level of resources (money, personnel, expertise) do I need for this project?
- *What standards?* What are the appropriate standards that are consistent with the information generated by the prior two questions?
- *Which standard?* Of these various standards, which is the most appropriate one to use and how does it align with the business model of my organization (value proposition, capabilities, and key customers)?
- *How to do it?* What is the process of achieving certification? Do I want to do it by myself or through a consultant? What intensity should I apply to this certification, that is, mandatory, quasimandatory, or voluntary?
- *What resources are available?* What resources can I draw on to achieve this level of certification?
- *What's next?* After I get certified, what am I going to do next?

Certification can be viewed as part of an ongoing process. If so, then there should be a next step and continuous improvement.

We have provided you many questions, but you, the reader, have the answers. The goals of sustainability standards are to provide a platform for insight as to what is important while leveraging best practices. Standards help to level the playing field for companies, as well as their customers, investors, employees, and others, in assessing what it means to be a sustainable business. Standards go a long way toward helping all stakeholders understand and assess a full spectrum of social and environmental issues of importance today.

The abovementioned standards are a starting place for the application of rules, guidelines, and structure for activities or the development of new systems. The resources provide the full documentation and metrics for assessing performance while also offering a means for certification (formal recognition that your organization has satisfied certain minimum sets of requirements prescribed by the standard). These standards by themselves are not enough. We have provided information on a diverse range of standards, including structure, sources, intensity, types, and use as benchmarks. These standards also need the support of a range of tools in order to better manage processes and outcomes that align with S^3CM. More information on available tools will be discussed in the next chapter.

Summary

This chapter has focused on those developments necessary if we are to begin implementing the sustainable supply chain. These developments include: standards and verification of a more dynamic understanding of processes, products, and services. What we have presented in this chapter can be summarized as follows:

Standards play an important role in a sustainable supply chain and can be used to achieve a number of important outcomes. While standards are not perfect instruments; they should be leveraged for their alignment with a given business model and used carefully. There are a large (and ever-growing) number of standards appropriate to sustainability along with a process for the appropriate usage and implementation of standards. The focus on standards is part of process thinking (where standards can be viewed as giving managers either process templates or standards for performance).

The sustainable supply chain can be achieved. We have the rationale for sustainability; we have the components; and, now, in Volume 1 (Foundations) and this chapter, we have the standards to help make sustainability a reality.

Applied Learning: Action Items (AIs)—Steps You Can Take to Apply the Learning From This Chapter

AI: What sustainability standards are used in your industry?

AI: What performance metrics are materials to your industry?

AI: What sustainability standards align with existing core capabilities and your business model?

AI: Find examples of integrated reporting from companies in Europe or the United States?

AI: What standards or certifications do you and your suppliers possess?

AI: What new markets can you enter if you become certified to a sustainability standard?

AI: Are you a good customer, and are your suppliers acting like good customers?

AI: Work through a mock supplier development project, pick a supplier, and propose how you would successfully deploy sustainability standards?

Further Readings

The International Integrated Reporting Council (IIRC). "The Integrated Reporting Journey: The Inside Story." http://integratedreporting.org/resource/the-integrated-reporting-journey-the-inside-story-2/.

Dentch, M. P. *The ISO 14001 Implementation Handbook: Using the Process Approach to Build an Environmental Management System.* ASQ Quality Press, 2016.

International Living Future Institute. "Living Product Challenge." https://living-future.org/lpc/.

Visser, W. *Landmarks for Sustainability: Events and Initiatives That Have Changed Our World.* Sheffield, UK: Greenleaf Publishing Limited, 2009.

Willard, B. *The New Sustainability Advantage.* Gabriola, BC: New Society Publishers, 2012.

CHAPTER 8

Tools in Support of S³CM

Our tools are better than we are, and grow faster than we do. They suffice to crack the atom, to command the tides. But they do not suffice for the oldest task in human history: to live on a piece of land without spoiling it.

—Aldo Leopold

Better management through tools and frameworks:

- The decisions of companies such as General Motors and Ford to include sustainability as corporate goals have led to the realization among many suppliers that developing an environmental management system and becoming ISO 14001 certified not only results in improvements in efficiency and profitability but that such certification also help suppliers retain their position in the original equipment manufacturer (OEM) supply chain. Furthermore, suppliers such as Texas Nameplate Co. (Dallas, TX) and Howard Plating Industries (Madison Heights, MI) have found that ISO 14001 certification has several tools supporting it and leads to a safer and healthier environment for their employees.
- Tools are available to help. Sustainability assessment and management have been recommended by the Committee on Incorporating Sustainability in the U.S. EPA for over two decades. It involves comprehensive and systems-based analysis of alternatives and options that integrate the evaluation of social, environmental, and economic consequences; intergenerational long-term consequences of alternatives in addition to

more immediate consequences; and stakeholder involvement and collaboration throughout the process.[*]

- In these vignettes, we see the Big Three automotive firms pushing for sustainability throughout their supply chain; the U.S. EPA ensuring available processes for sustainability assessment based on process tools and indicators; and a burgeoning amount of standards, tools, and practices available to help managers take on new initiatives. In these instances, the firms involved turned to sustainability standards and tools to find solutions. Standards, while important, are only one of many tools available to managers who want to make their supply chains sustainable. Because we cannot cover all of them, we will focus our attention on critical tools that every manager should consider and use.

Objectives

1. Look at process thinking and process flow analysis.
2. Review available quality management tools already supporting sustainability.
3. Understand how to apply problem-solving approaches and process tools to sustainability.

Tools: Process Thinking and Process Flow Analysis

Sustainability can be viewed as an output resulting from various processes. Some of these processes take place in design, in production, and others in delivery, usage, disposal, or closed-loop systems. A supply chain can be regarded as simply a set of processes. Why is this focus on processes so important? Because it leads to a simple but important perspective: *if you don't like the outcome, change the processes.* In other words, if you are not getting the level and type of sustainability that you want in the supply chain, you have to identify the processes responsible

[*]Sustainability and the U.S. EPA (2011). Chapter 4 Sustainability Assessment and Management: Process, Tools, and Indicators; National Academies Press; www.nap.edu/read/13152/chapter/6.

for the problems, study them, and then change them. This perspective is more commonly referred to as process thinking and is a complement to both systems thinking and design thinking.

Process thinking is a way of viewing activities in an organization as a collection of processes (as opposed to departments or functional areas). This way of thinking focuses management's attention not only on the outputs but also on the processes responsible for these outcomes. At the heart of process thinking is Juran's Law. Joseph Juran (1904 to 2008) was one of the leading quality gurus of the 20th century. He once observed that *15 percent of operational problems result from human error; the other 85 percent are due to systematic process errors.* Accordingly, if we are to pursue sustainability, we should focus our attention on processes.

Because processes spread across many organizations that make up the supply chain, it is important for all managers at all levels and in all major departments to understand the basic operating principles of process thinking. One way of expressing these principles is through a management system known as the theory of constraints (TOC).[†] The principles present in the TOC are universally applicable, whether the processes are in a manufacturing plant, a service facility, a sales office, a hospital, or in a financial planning office.

These principles simplify process management and process thinking by focusing management's attention on the important constraints that limit the performance of a process. There are five basic principles underlying the TOC:

1. Every process has a constraint.
2. Every process contains variance that consumes capacity.
3. Every process must be managed as a system.
4. Every process's performance measures are critical to overall success.
5. Every process must continually improve.

Of these five, we will focus attention on the last. This principle emphasizes the fact that we are living in a dynamic world. Technology

---

[†]TOC was initially developed and presented by Eli Goldratt. His popular book, *The Goal* (1984), explains the basic principles in the context of a fictional story.

Table 8.1 Six types of critical processes

Process type	Why critical
Bottleneck	Limits output; increases lead time; adversely affects cost, quality, flexibility, increases risk, and ultimately impacts sustainability.
Visible to the customer	Affects how the customer views not only the process but also the firm's reputation and brand if supply chains contain human rights violations, lack social accountability, or have detrimental impacts on the environment.
Core capability	A process that incorporates a critical strategic skillset that is difficult for the competition to copy. It must be guarded, managed, and improved continuously because it is the major source of the firm's value. Every firm should be able to identify its core capabilities and align these with sustainability initiatives.
Feeder processes	A process that feeds several alternative processes coming out of it. A problem in this process (e.g., a delay or a quality problem) could affect the many resulting processes.
Greatest variance	Variances are amplified by sequential steps in processes. To reduce variances, managers should identify the steps that cause the greatest variance and continuously work toward reducing them.
Most resources consumed	We focus on these processes because they offer the "biggest bang for the buck," and are directly tied to process waste, GHG emissions, carbon, and future risks. They also contain integrated management opportunities for greater efficiency and effectiveness.

(big data analytics, IoT, GenAI) is always changing; the competition is changing, and customers (and their expectations) are also changing. Consequently, processes (especially critical processes, as identified in Table 8.1) should also change. They must be evaluated and change when the level of value they provide is no longer acceptable to key customers or management.

There are several specific tools that can be used to aid process improvement efforts, including process flow analysis, value stream, mapping, and Kaizen events. There is a vast amount of information outside this book available to readers about each of the following sections. Instead of trying to reference all this information, we provide a succinct summary, and we leave it to the reader to learn more about these additional procedures and tools.

Consider for a moment process flow analysis. This technique is used for documenting activities in a detailed, compact, and graphic form to help managers understand processes and highlight areas for potential improvements. Process flow analysis generates a process blueprint that supplies nearly all the information needed to effectively assess a process, with the goal of answering the following critical questions: *Does the existing process make the desired outcome inevitable? If not, what must be done to create a process that makes the desired outcome inevitable?*

Process flow analysis itself is based on a process consisting of six critical steps:

1. Determine the desired outcome for the entire process and the associated sustainability metrics needed to evaluate that process's performance. Identify and set boundaries for the critical process.
2. Identify and set boundaries for the critical process.
3. Document the existing process (to determine the "current state" map).
4. Analyze the process and prioritize opportunities for improvement.
5. Recommend appropriate changes to the process (aimed at achieving the "future state" map).
6. Implement the changes and monitor improvements.

These six steps are as readily applicable to improving sustainability in the supply chain as they are to helping the firm reduce costs, improve quality, and reduce lead times.

In addition to process flow analysis, there is also *value stream mapping*. This technique analyzes the flow of material and information currently needed to bring a product to a customer. Value stream mapping is used to assess the extent to which the current process adds value (as a percentage of the total time) and to identify opportunities for reducing lead time and cost and attaining such outcomes as sustainability. It is more comprehensive and complex than process flow analysis.

Quality Management Tools

Quality management tools have been a staple of most firms' systems since the mid-1980s when the importance of quality was forcefully introduced to American management by quality gurus such as Deming, Juran, Crosby, and Imai. That is when most firms were introduced to the concept of total quality management (TQM). At that time, we were introduced to the importance of quality both as a tactical and strategic imperative (i.e., quality not only affected the dollars and cents but also it also affected how the firm competes). We were also introduced to the tools and the process of problem-solving under TQM. These tools and processes are the same that today should be extended to sustainability and supply chain management.

The approach to problems taken by TQM formed a natural complement to the process-thinking orientation discussed in the preceding section. That is, quality problems are the results of processes. We can focus on correcting the problems as they are generated by the process, in which case we are perpetually engaged in continuous corrective action. AND, we can identify the underlying reasons for the problems, focus on the processes responsible for these root causes, and then take action to change the processes to bring about the desired outcomes. This approach, often referred to as Quality at the Source, or Q@S, argues that those who create the problem are responsible for preventing the problem. This approach seeks to prevent problems from occurring in the first place rather than simply correcting them once they are created. This same approach (with its emphasis on process thinking and prevention rather than correction) is also highly appropriate when dealing with the goals of social equity and minimizing environmental impacts in the supply chain.

Underlying this approach is the view that achieving an outcome such as improved sustainability or quality is a never-ending quest. Products, processes, and customer expectations are always changing. Consequently, we are always working on meeting these new, changing needs. To help us survive in this dynamic environment, we can draw on the overall problem-solving approaches of quality management and various quality management tools.

The Overall Problem-Solving Approach

While there are many problem-solving and project-development approaches, we will focus on two of the most well-known, the Plan-Do-Check-Act Cycle (PDCA, otherwise known as the Deming Wheel) and Define, Measure, Analyze, Improve, and Control (DMAIC) from Six Sigma.

Deming's Plan-Do-Check-Act Cycle

This approach (also called the PDCA cycle) was first developed by Dr. Deming. It emphasized the ongoing nature of problem-solving by identifying four processes that are linked in an endless cycle:

1. Plan: The first step is to identify the problem by studying the current situation. Identify the nature of the gap that separates where we are from and where we want to be. Identify the reasons for this gap and the processes responsible for this gap. Once this is done, formulate specific actions intended to close this gap.
2. Do: Having developed the plan, now implement it.
3. Check: Use metrics (previously discussed in Chapter 3) to monitor the progress of the actions deployed in the preceding step. Determine if these actions are achieving the desired results. Also, we need to determine whether we are encountering any unplanned problems in the system—problems that were previously hidden.
4. Act: Review the information collected in the Check step and take corrective actions to prevent problems from reoccurring. Also, during this stage, institutionalize changes (through standards, revised procedures, and associated training). With the insights and information gained during this stage, you are ready to repeat the process by returning to the Plan step of a new PDCA cycle.

The major advantage and attraction of PDCA cycle is that it is simple. It gives all employees, both within the firm and the supply chain, a structure for attacking problems on a daily basis. By being simple, it can be easily taught to and readily understood by all employees within the system.

DMAIC

DMAIC, a key element of the Six Sigma process of TQM, can be viewed as a further refinement and extension of the PDCA cycle.

DMAIC is taken from the first letter of the five steps that make up this process:

- Define: The first step is to understand the task and problem facing the team. This requires generating a problem statement, identification of the key customers, flagging *critical to quality* (CTQ—the critical process outcomes), determining the critical processes, and then bounding these processes. The goal of this first step is to develop a thorough understanding of what is required.
- Measure: At the heart of this second step is data collection. Having identified the critical processes that influence CTQ, the team now collects data to better understand what is going on in these processes.
- Analyze: The resulting data is then analyzed to determine the root causes of the resulting variance and problems.
- Improve: The intent in this step is to generate solutions aimed at correcting and fixing the root causes previously identified.
- Control: The final step is to put actions and tools in place necessary to keep the processes operating appropriately. This means updating process documents, business processes, and training records as needed.

DMAIC is a very data-driven process that extensively uses a portfolio of quality management tools.

Quality Management Tools Supporting Sustainability

What TQM offers the manager interested in developing a strategic sustainable supply chain is a rich, proven set of tools. It is important to

Table 8.2 Major quality management tools

Quality tool	Typical usage
Cause and effect analysis	A critical tool (everyone who is engaged in the drive to a strategic sustainable supply chain should have a working knowledge of this tool). Helps uncover possible factors contributing to an observed problem (as well as the possible structure). Encourages group brainstorming. Prevents the onset of myopic management (e.g., "I know what the problem is; don't confuse me with facts").
Histogram	Helps uncover underlying patterns (range and frequency) in the observed data.
Check sheets	Helps identify the frequency and location of problem causes.
Pareto analysis	Another critical tool. Helps identify the most critical causes of observed problems. Becomes a prioritized list for action.
Scatter diagrams	Helps determine if two variables are related to each other (do the two variables move together in some predictable manner).
Process flow analysis	Another critical tool. Graphically displays and analyzes steps in a process.
Process capability analysis	Helps predict the conformance quality of a product by comparing its specification range to the range of its process variability.
Process control charts	Helps monitor process outputs and determine whether a process is operating within normally expected limits.
Taguchi method/ design of experiments	Helps evaluate and understand the effects of different factors on process outputs.

recognize that these tools are not simply for quality problems. Rather, these tools should be viewed as management tools—tools that are useful for addressing any form of management problem and necessary decision making. Table 8.2 provides a summary of the major tools and their usage.

In reviewing Table 8.2, it is important to note that we have flagged certain tools as more critical than others. This designation is based on the author's experience in this field. The tools in bold type are the ones for which it is important that management gain a good understanding and mastery before they proceed into any process improvement project.

We next want to introduce a tool outside of the quality management domain, yet very useful to the application of decision making for emerging sustainability practices involving multiple criteria and alternatives.

Multiple-criteria Decision Analysis

Multiple-criteria decision analysis (MCDA) methods have become increasingly popular in decision making for sustainable business practices because of the multidimensionality of sustainability goals and the complexity of social, environmental, and economic performance. We propose the use of the analytic hierarchy process (AHP) as an MCDA tool for helping managers structure the problem of integrating social and environmental dimensions into process improvement projects, supplier evaluation, and selection decisions, resolving trade-offs, and to better screen and assess supplier performance.[2] AHP is a simple yet powerful decision support tool developed within the management science field decades ago.[3] It was developed to help managers make more effective decisions by structuring and evaluating the relative attractiveness of competing options or alternatives. The AHP has been used successfully for structuring decision making in many areas of business management and planning. To briefly describe this approach, AHP requires the decision maker to describe up to four different components: the objective, the relevant criteria, the relevant subcriteria, if any, and the alternatives to be evaluated. One major advantage of AHP is that constructing a hierarchy diagram forces the decision maker to structure the problem. Requiring the decision maker to explicitly define the objective and relevant criteria and assign numerical values for their relative importance forces the decision maker to consider trade-offs in detail. Since managers typically rely on only a subset of information (e.g., heuristics), AHP helps managers make "more rational" decisions by structuring the decision as they see it and then fully considering all available information on the criteria and alternatives. In other words, developing the AHP model provides value on its own in understanding sustainability criteria and alternatives, independent of the final ranked evaluation of the alternatives.

Building on What We Know

This chapter can be viewed as having a "bad news/good news" message. The bad news is that we must draw on a large set of standards, tools, and procedures to help us in the challenge of making the strategic supply chain efficient and sustainable. The good news is that many of these tools and procedures are already in place. If you or your firm has implemented systems such as Lean/JIT, or TQM, or Six Sigma, then it is very likely that you already have in place the tools needed to help make the supply chain not only more efficient but also more sustainable. Add to this management toolkit MCDA methods, and decision makers can better assess the multidimensionality of existing and emerging sustainability opportunities. Consequently, this chapter argues that you should leverage your knowledge of these tools and apply them to the task of making your supply chain sustainable.

Leveraging existing sustainability standards and quality management tools provides a good foundation for new initiatives and should be applied whenever possible because it builds on what you currently know and understand. We do not have to reinvent the wheel regarding sustainable practices. Instead, we can utilize known standards and tools as best practices to more quickly cross the chasm on a path to better social equity, less environmental impacts, AND improved economic performance. Leveraging standards and tool, along with collaboration with stakeholders up and down a supply chain helps reduce confusion, training time, and resistance to change. It also reduces the total time and cost needed for the transformation.

Summary

This chapter has focused on process thinking and process tools, along with quality management tools and processes. What we have presented so far, and in this chapter, can be summarized as follows:

Our focus on standards enables process thinking (where standards can be viewed as giving managers either process templates or standards for performance). Process thinking argues that every outcome or output (where sustainability is simply another form of outcome) is the result of a process. If you don't like the output, you must identify the processes responsible for it and focus your attention on them. Process thinking is enabled by tools such as process flow analysis, value stream mapping, and frameworks such as the TOC. You, as a manager, and other decision makers in your organization can draw on the problem-solving frameworks developed in the quality management field (specifically the PDCA and the DMAIC of Six Sigma). These frameworks are widely accepted and recognized to be effective for continuous improvement and as a foundation for integrating strategic sustainability into any organization. Furthermore, managers can draw on the well-developed tools of quality management—tools such as cause-and-effect analysis, pareto analysis, and histogram—to get a better idea of what is taking place within the system (what the nature of the problems are, where they are located, and factors contributing to these problems). This information can be taken a step further to inform cash flow analysis, the modeling of uncertainty and outcomes with simulations, and new insights as to what variables related to sustainability have the largest impacts on financial outcomes, including SVA.

In most cases, the tools, frameworks, and procedures discussed in this chapter are not new to the firm. They have been implemented because of developments such as TQM, and Lean/JIT. What is needed is for the firm to leverage these elements and to reapply them with a focus on making a supply chain sustainable.

The strategic sustainable supply chain can be achieved. We have the rationale for sustainability; we have the components; and, now, in Volume 1 (Foundations) and this chapter, we have the tools, and frameworks to make sustainability a reality.

We hope you continue reading and exploring new opportunities for action learning in Volume 2 (Implementation), where we will review the following:

- Chapter 1: Design for Sustainability
- Chapter 2: S³CMFrameworks and Tools
- Chapter 3: Integration—Supply Chain Management and Sustainability
- Chapter 4: Achieving Integration—Enabling Stakeholders and Customers.
- Chapter 5: Sustainable Systems—Order Winners of the Future along with an extended look at Aura Lighting's Application of the Framework for Strategic Sustainability Development to their Supply Chain
- Chapter 6: Implementing S³CM to Drive Value
- Chapter 7: Strategic Sustainable Supply Chain Management—The End of the Beginning

Applied Learning: Action Items (AIs)—Steps You Can Take to Apply the Learning From This Chapter

AI: Which process management tools are in use within your company?

AI: To what extent do management systems support process management?

AI: What sustainability tools and frameworks are used in your industry?

AI: Which sustainability tools support existing core capabilities and your business model?

AI: To what extent does your company have a formal environmental management system in place and how long has it been in place?

AI: To what extent can you use MCDA to prioritize new sustainability initiatives and supporting tools?

AI: How will advances in technology, that is , Blockchain, IoT, Industry 4.0, and GenAI, be used as tools to impact your ability to understand process management?

Further Readings

Awan, U., R. Sroufe, and M. Shahbaz. "Industry 4.0 and The Circular Economy: A Literature Review and Recommendations for Future Research." *Business Strategy and the Environment* 30, no. 4 (2021): 2038–2060.

KEK, V., S. Rajak, V. Kumar, R. Mor, and A. Assayed. *Industry 4.0 Technologies: Sustainable Manufacturing Supply Chains.* Springer Nature, 2023.

McCarty, T., M. Jordan and D. Probst. *Six Sigma for Sustainability.* NY, New York: McGraw Hill, 2011.

Mubarik, M. and M. Shahbaz. *Blockchain Driven Supply Chain Management.* Springer, 2023.

Stanislawski, R and A. Szymonik. *Supply Chains in Reverse Logistics—The Process Approach for Sustainability and Environmental Protection.* Routledge, 2024.

UNGC and BSR Supply Chain Sustainability: A Practical Guide to Continusous Improvement. 2010. www.bsr.org/reports/BSR_UNGC_SupplyChainReport.pdf.

Notes

Chapter 1

1. International Institute for Sustainable Development (2024).
2. MIT Sloan Management Review and Boston Consulting Group, "Sustainability Nears a Tipping Point: Findings From the 2011 Sustainability and Innovation Global Executive Study and Research Report."
3. McKinsey," Global Survey Results."
4. GlobeScan/Salesforce, "Value of Sustainability Project."
5. Shrivastava (2007).
6. Meadows, *Thinking in Systems: A Primer.*
7. Broman and Robért, "A Framework for Strategic Sustainable Development," 17–31.
8. Sroufe, (2025) *Integrated Management: How Sustainability Creates Value for any Business.*
9. Accenture, "The Sustainable Supply Chain."
10. Ibid.
11. Eccles, Ioannou and Serafeim, "The Impact of a Corporate Culture of Sustainability on Corporate Behavior and Performance."
12. McDonough and Braungart, *Cradle to Cradle.*
13. McDonough, W., and Braungart, M. (2013).
14. Deloitte, "Comprehensive Analysis of the SEC's Landmark Climate Disclosure Rule."

Chapter 2

1. Forbes, "U.S. Natural Disasters Cost $145 Billion Last Year."
2. Procurement Intelligence Unit, "By Procurement Intelligence Staff."
3. Craft, "Envisioning a Smarter, Healthier Supply Chain for Shippers."
4. Ibid.
5. 2020 Future Value Chain Project.
6. Lubin and Esty, "The Sustainability Imperative," 43–45.
7. Porter and Kramer, "Creating Shared Value," 62–77.

8. Nattrass and Altomare, *The Natural Step for business: Wealth, Ecology and the Evolutionary Corporation.*

9. Broman and Robert.

10. Missimer, Robsrt, and Broman. "Lessons From The Field: A First Evaluation of Working With the Elaborated Social Dimensions of the Framework for Strategic Sustainable Development."

11. Sroufe, "Operationalizing Sustainability."

12. Bronman and Robèrt, "A Framework for Strategic Sustainable Development."

13. França et al., "An Approach to Business Model Innovation and Design for Strategic Sustainable Development."

14. Ibid.

Chapter 3

1. McKinsey & Company, "Consumers Care About Sustainability—and Back it up With Their Wallets."

2. Ignatius, "Unilever CEO Paul Polman," 115.

3. Ibid.

4. SLDI.

5. Eccles and Krzus, *One Report-Integrated Reporting for a Sustainable Strategy.*

6. Scott, "100 Most Sustainable Companies of 2023 Still Flourishing in Tumultuous Times."

7. Annie, The Story of Stuff.

8. Lovins, Lovins and Hawkins, *Natural Capitalism.*

9. Starbucks, "Responsibly Grown Coffee."

10. Schwarz, "Best Brands for Social Impact."

11. Phipps, "Ten Worst Companies in terms of Social and Environmental Responsibility."

12. KPMG, "Sustainability Reporting-What You Should Know."; KPMG "The Corporate Sustainability Progress Report."

Chapter 4

1. Jones and Roos, *The Machine That Changed the World.*

2. Lawrence Livermore National Laboratory, "Estimated U.S. Energy Consumption for 2022, Energy, Water, and Carbon Informatics."

3. Eccles and Taylor, "The Evolving Role of Chief Sustainability Officers."

4. Melnyk et al., "Outcome Driven Supply Chains," 33–38.

5. Hill, *Manufacturing Strategy: Text and Cases.*

6. MIT Sloan Management Review and Boston Consulting Group, "The Innovation Bottom Line."

7. Jana, *Business Week,* 48.

8. Chesbrough and Rosenbloom, "The Role of the Business Model in Capturing Value From Innovation: Evidence From Xerox Corporation's Technology Spin-Off Companies," 525–559.

9. Markides (1998).

10. Melnyk et al., "Outcome Driven Supply Chains," 33–38.

11. Figge, Hahn, and Tobias, "Sustainable Value Added—Measuring Corporate Contributions to Sustainability Beyond Eco-Efficiency," 173–187.

12. Puma Press Kit, Puma Completes first Environmental Profit and Loss Account Which Values Impacts at € 145M.

13. Kohli and Leuthesser, "Brand Equity: Capitalizing on Intellectual Capital."

14. Natural Capitalism Solutions, "Sustainability Pays: Studies That Prove the Business Case for Sustainability."

Chapter 5

1. EPA, *The Social Cost of Carbon.*

2. IMF, "More Countries Are Pricing Carbon, but Emissions Are Still Too Cheap."

3. Magretta and Stone (2002).

4. Willard, *The New Sustainability Advantage.*

5. Blackburn, *The Sustainability Handbook,* 17–33.

6. Lovins and Cohen, 25–26.

7. Sroufe, "Operationalizing Sustainability."

8. FedEx Global Citizen Report.

9. UPS, "Sustainability at UPS Report."

10. Berthelot et al., "Environmental Disclosure Research: Review and Synthesis," 1–44; KPMG, "Sustainable Insight-Your Quarterly Insight Into Sustainability."

11. Lambert and Pohlen, "Supply Chain Metrics," 1–19.

12. Porter and Kramer, "Creating Shared Value," 62–77.

13. Culture Map, "9 Metrics to Help You Understand (and Prioritize) DEI."

Chapter 6

1. KPMG, "Survey of Sustainability."
2. Brown et al., *The Rise of the Global Reporting Initiative (GRI) as a Case of Institutional Entrepreneurship,* 1–48.
3. Carbon Disclosure Project, "CDP Supply Chain Report."

Chapter 7

1. PWC, "The SEC's Climate Disclosure Rules Are the Latest to Require Expanded."
2. DuPont, "Sustainability Goals."
3. Melnyk, Peters, Schoenherr, and Miller, "Earned Preferential Treatment: The Reward for Being a "Good" Customer," 40–47.

Chapters 8

1. Sustainability and the U.S. EPA, "4 Sustainability Assessment and Management: Process, Tools, and Indicators."
2. Handfield (2002).
3. Saaty, "How to Make a Decision—The Analytic Hierarchy Process," 9–26.

References

This list includes both references that were directly cited in this Volume and useful references. Any reference denoted by a *, if not directly cited in this text, is useful and it should be read because it contributes to a better understanding of the issues raised in this two Volume set regarding S3CM.

Accenture. *The sustainable supply chain*. 2009. Retrieved March 22, 2013. www.accenture.com.

*Allenby, B. *Industrial Ecology*. New York, NY: Prentice Hall, 1993.

Awan, U., R. Sroufe, and M. Shahbaz, M. "Industry 4.0 and The Circular Economy: A Literature Review and Recommendations for Future Research," *Business Strategy and the Environment* 30, no. 4 (2021): 2038–2060.

Berthelot, S., D. Cormier, and M. Magnan. "Environmental Disclosure Research: Review and Synthesis," *Journal of Accounting Literature* 22 (2003): 1–44.

*Bhat, V. "Green Marketing Begins With Green Design." *Journal of Business and Industrial Marketing* 8, no. 3 (1993): 26–31.

Blackburn, W. "Determining Scope: An Operational Definition of Sustainability," Chapter 2, *The Sustainability Handbook*, 17–33. Washington DC: Environmental Law Institute, Eli Press, 2016.

*Branchfeld, D., T. Dritz, S. Kodaman, A. Phipps, E. Steiner, and G. Keoleian. *Life Cycle Assessment of the Stonyfield Product Delivery System*. Ann Arbor: University of Michigan. Master's Thesis, CSS01-03, 2001.

*Bratt, C. *Integrating A Strategic Sustainability Perspective Into Ecolabeling, Procurement, and Supply Chain Management*, Doctoral dissertation series No. 2014:06, Blekinge Institute of Technology, Department of Strategic Sustainable Development, Karlskrona, Sweden. 2014.

*Braumguart, M., and M. McDonough. "Cradle to Cradle Design: Creating Healthy Emissions—A Strategy for Eco-Effective Product and System Design." *Journal of Cleaner Production* 15 (2007):1337–1348.

*Broman, G. I., and K.-H. Robért. "A Framework for Strategic Sustainable Development." *Journal of Cleaner Production* 140 (2017): 17–31.

Brown, H. S., D. J. Martin, and L. Teodorina. *The Rise of the Global Reporting Initiative (GRI) as a Case of Institutional Entrepreneurship*. Harvard University, 2007. 1–48. www.hks.harvard.edu. September 22, 2011. Retrieved March 22, 2013. www.hks.harvard.edu/mrcbg/CSRI/publications/workingpaper_36_brown.pdf.

Carbon Disclosure Project. Retrieved September 27, 2011. www.cdproject.net/en-US//Pages/overview.aspx.

Carbon Disclosure Project. *CDP Supply Chain Report 2012.* 2012. Retrieved March 22, 2013. www.cdproject.net/CDPResults/CDP-Supply-Chain-Report-2012.pdf.

*Carbon Disclosure Project & Accenture. *Reducing Risk and Driving Business Value—DCP Supply Chain Report.* 2012. Retrieved March 22, 2013. www.cdproject.net/CDPResults/CDP-Supply-Chain-Report 2013.pdf.

Carbon Disclosure Project (CDP). *Putting a Price on Carbon,* 2021. Retrieve May 29, 2024. https://cdn.cdp.net/cdp-production/cms/reports/documents/000/005/651/original/CDP_Global_Carbon_Price_report_2021.pdf?1618938446.

*Charan, P., R. Shankar, and R. K. Baisya. "Analysis of Interactions Among the Variables of Supply Chain Performance Measurement System Implementation." *Business Process Manage Journal* 14, no. 4 (2008): 512–529.

Chesbrough, H., and Rosenbloom, R. S. "The Role of the Business Model in Capturing Value From Innovation: Evidence From Xerox Corporation's Technology Spin-Off Companies." *Industrial and Corporate Change,* 11, no. (3) 2002, 529–555.

CNN Money. "Forbes' Most Admired Companie: The Top Ten and Worst for Social Performance," from the March 2012 issue, 2012. Retrieved, July 16, 2012. http://money.cnn.com/magazines/fortune/most-admired/2012/best_worst/ best4.html.

Culture Map. "9 Metrics to Help You Understand (and prioritize) DEI," 2024. Retrieved May 29, 2024. www.cultureamp.com/blog/dei-metrics#:~:text=What%20are%20DEI%20metrics%3F,create%20a%20definition%20of%20success.

*Curkovic, S., and R. P. Sroufe. "Using ISO 14001 to Promote A Sustainable Supply Chain Strategy." *Business Strategy and the Environment* 20 (2011): 71–93.

*Deloitte. *The millennial survey,* 2011. Retrieved March 28, 2013. www.deloitte.com/view/en_GX/global/about/business-society/7db3b035c93d4310VgnVCM2000001b56f00aRCRD.htm#.UVnOFzdc3vg.

Deloitte. "Comprehensive Analysis o the SEC's Landmark Climate Disclosure Rule." 2024. Retrieved May 28. https://dart.deloitte.com/USDART/home/publications/deloitte/heads-up/2024/sec-climate-disclosure-rule-ghg-emissions-esg-financial-reporting.

*DHL. *Corporate Responsibility Report,* 2011. Retrieved March 22, 2013, www.dhl.com/content/dam/downloads/g0/about_us/DPDHL_CR%20Report_2011.pdf.

DuPont. "2015 Sustainability Goals—DuPont Footprint." *DuPont: The Miracles of Science*, 2010. Retrieved January 2, 2010. www2.dupont.com/Sustainability/en_US/Footprint/index.html.

Eccles, R. G., and M. P. Krzus. *One Report-Integrated Reporting for a Sustainable Strategy.* Hoboken. New Jersey: Wiley & Sons, Inc, 2010.

Eccles, R. G., I. Ioannou, and G. Serafeim. "The Impact of a Corporate Culture of Sustainability on Corporate Behavior and Performance." *Harvard Working Paper*, 2011. Retrieved March 22, 2013. http://hbswk.hbs.edu/item/6865.html.

*Ehrenfeld, J. *Sustainability by Design.* New Haven: Yale University Press, 2008.

*Elkington, J. *Green swans: the coming boom in regenerative capitalism.* Greenleaf Book Group, 2020.

ELM Consulting Group. "OECD to SEC: Make Us the Conflict Minerals Due Diligence/Audit Standard for the US | Your EHS Connection," *Elmconsultinggroup.wordpress.com*, 2011. July 7, 2011. Retrieved February 8, 2013. http://elmconsultinggroup.wordpress.com/2011/07/07/oecd-to-sec-make-us-the-conflict-minerals-due-diligenceaudit-standard-for-the-us/.

EPA. Social Cost of Carbon. "Estimating the Benefits of Reducing Greenhouse Gas Emissions"; Retrieved May 29, 2024 from FedEx Global Citizen Report (2023). Retrieved May 29, 2024, https://s21.q4cdn.com/665674268/files/doc_downloads/2023/10/30/2023-FedEx-Economic-Impact-Report.pdf.

EPA Chapter 4 Sustainability Assessment and Management: Process, Tools, and Indicators; National Academies Press; Retrieved May 29, 2024 from www.nap.edu/read/13152/chapter/6.2011.

Figge, F., and Hahn, T. "Sustainable Value Added—Measuring Corporate Contributions to Sustainability Beyond Eco-Efficiency." *Ecological Economics* 48, no. 2 (2004): 173–187.

Franca, C. L. *Introductory Approach to Business Model Design for Strategic Sustainable Development*, Doctoral dissertation series No. 2013:08, Blekinge Institute of Technology, Department of Strategic Sustainable Development, Karlskrona, Sweden, 2013.

*Franca, C. L., G. Broman., K-H. Robért., G. Basile and L. Trygg. "An Approach to Business Model Innovation and Design for Strategic Sustainable Development." *Journal of Cleaner Production* 140 (2017): 155–166.

*Frosch, R. A., and N. E. Gallopoulos. "Strategies for Manufacturing." *Scientific American* 261, (1989): 144–152.

*Gallop. *The Relationship Between Engagement at Work and Organizational Outcomes.* 2009. Retrieved January 20, 2012. www.gallop.com/consulting/126806/Q-12-Meta-Analysis.aspx.

Global 100. *The Global 100 Most Sustainable Corporations in the World.* 2012. Retrieved July 11, 2012. www.global100.org/annual-lists/2012-global-100 -list.html.

*Global Reporting Initiative. 2024. Retrieved May 29, 2024. www. globalreporting.org/.

GlobeScan/Salesforce. *Value of Sustainability project.* Retrieved May 28, 2024. from https://globescan.com/2024/02/29/insight-of-the-week-where-sustainability- is-bringing-value/.

*Goldratt, E. *The Goal.* Great Barrington, MA: North River Press. 1984.

GreenSCOR. *Upgrading the SCOR Model to Include Social and Environmental Factors,* 2024. Retrieved May 29, 2024. https://majorsustainability.smeal. psu.edu/greenscor-model/.

*Grzybowska, K. "Sustainability in the Supply Chain: Analysis of Enablers," Chapter 2 within Golinska, P and C. A. Romano (eds.), *Environmental Issues in Supply Chain Management, EcoProduction.* Berlin Heidelberg: Springer- Verlag. doi: 10.1007/978-3-642-23562-7_2.

Handfield, R., S. V. Walto, R. P. Sroufe, and S. A. Melnyk. (2002). "Applying Environmental Criteria to Supplier Assessment: A Study in the Application of the Analytical Hierarchy Process." *European Journal of Operational Research* 141 (2002), 70–87.

Hawken, P. (Ed.). *Drawdown: The Most Comprehensive Plan Ever Proposed to Reverse Global Warming.* Penguin, 2017.

*Henderson, R. M. *Reimagining Capitalism in a World on Fire, Public Affairs,* NY, NY, 2020.

Henderson, R. M. "Reimagining Capitalism." *Management and Business Review* 1, no. 1 (2021). Retrieved May 29, 2024. https://mbrjournal.com/2020/12/23/ reimagining-capitalism/.

*Hawkins, P., A. Lovins, and H. Lovins. *Natural Capitalism.* Little, Brown and Company. Boston, New York and London, 2008.

*Hawks, K. "VP Supply Chain Practice, Navesink." *Reverse Logistics Magazine* Winter/Spring, 2006. Retrieved March 28, 2013. www.rlmagazine.com/ edition01p12.php.

*Henretig, J. "Up in the Air, Director of environmental sustainability, Microsoft," *Sustainable industries,* March 2012, Retrieved March 22, 2013, www. sustainableindustries.com/articles/2012/03/air.

Hill, T. *Manufacturing Strategy: Text and Cases.* New York: McGraw-Hill/Irwin. 2000.

*Huang, Y. A., C. L. Weber, and H. S. Mathews. "Categorization of Scope Three Emissions for Streamlined Enterprise Carbon Footprinting." *Environmental Science Technology* 43, no. 22 (2009): 8509–8515.

Ignatius, A. "Unilever CEO Paul Polman: Captain Planet." *Harvard Business Review*, 112–118, 2012.

International Monetary Fund (IMF). "More Countries Are Pricing Carbon, but Emissions are Still Too Cheap," 2022. www.imf.org/en/Blogs/Articles/2022/07/21/blog-more-countries-are-pricing-carbon-but-emissions-are-still-too-cheap.

Intergovernmental Panel on Climate Change. *Sixth Assessment Report, Chapter 11 Industry Impacts.* 2023 Retrieved May 29, 2024. www.ipcc.ch/report/ar6/wg3/chapter/chapter-11/2023

International Institute for Sustainable Development. 2024. Retrieved May 22, 2024. www.iisd.org/sd/.

*International Living Future Institute. https://living-future.org/.

Jana, R. "Innovation: The Biggest Bang for the Buck." *Indata*, September 22, 48. 2008.

*Jensen, A. A., and A. Remmen. *Background Report for a UNEP Guide to Life Cycle Management—A Bridge to Sustainable Products*, 2006. Retrieved April 12, 2011. http://lcinitiative.unep.fr/includes/file.aspsite=lcinit&file=86E47576-EC54-4440-99B6-D6829EAF3622.

KEK, V., S. Rajak, V. Kumar, R. Mor, and A. Assayed. *Industry 4.0 Technologies: Sustainable Manufacturing Supply Chains.* Springer Nature, 2023.

Kohli, C., and L. Leuthesser L. *Brand Equity: Capitalizing on Intellectual Capital, 2001.* Retrieved December 20, 2012. www.iveybusinessjournal.com/.

Kollmus, A., H. Zink, and C. Polycarp. *Making Sense of the Voluntary Carbon Market: A Comparison of Carbon Offset Standards.* Stockholm Environmental Institute, World Wildlife Fund, 2008. Retrieved March 28, 2013. www.globalcarbonproject.org/global/pdf/WWF_2008_A%20comparison%20of%20C%20offset%20Standards.pdf.

KPMG. Sustainable Insight-Your Quarterly Insight into Sustainability, "Integrated reporting-closing the loop of strategy," KPMG Global Sustainability Services, 2010. www.scribd.com/document/315131381/Integrated-Reporting-Closing-the-Loop-of-Strategy.

KPMG. *Sustainability Reporting-What You Should Know.* 2011a. Retrieved March 28, 2013. www.kpmg.com/US/en/IssuesAndInsights/ArticlesPublications/Documents/iarcs-sustainability-reporting-what-you-should-know.pdf.

KPMG. *The Corporate Sustainability Progress Report.* 2011b. Retrieved March 22, 2013. www.kpmg.com/global/en/issuesandinsights/articlespublications/pages/corporate-sustainability.aspx.

Lambert, D., and T. Pohlen. "Supply Chain Metrics." *International Journal of Logistics Management* 12, no. 1 (2001): 1–19.

Lawrence Livermore National Laboratory. "Estimated U.S. Energy Consumption for 2022," *Energy, Water, and Carbon Informatics,* 2022. Retrieved May 29. https://flowcharts.llnl.gov/.

Lovins, A. B., L. H. Lovins, and P. Hawkins. "A Roadmap for Natural Capitalism." *Harvard Business Review* 85 (2003), 172–183.

Lovins, H., and B. Cohen. *The Way Out: Kick-Starting Capitalism to Save Our Economic Ass.* New York, NY: Hill & Wang, 2011.

*Lubber, M. "Compensation and Sustainability." *Harvard Business Review* 21, (2010), April 2010.

Lubin, D., and D. Esty. "The Sustainability Imperative." *Harvard Business Review* (2010): 43–5.

Magretta, J., and N. Stone. *What Management Is: How it Works and Why it's Everyone's Business.* New York, NY: Free Press, 2002.

Markides, C. "Strategic Innovation in Established Companies." *Sloan Management Review* 39, no. 3 (1998): 31–42.

*Mathews, H. S., C. Hendrickson, and C. L. Weber. "The Importance of Carbon Footprint Estimation Bounds." *Environmental Science Technology* 42, no. 16 (2008): 5839–5842.

*McDonald Corporation. *Global Best of Green 2012: Building a Better Business Through Effective Practices Around the World,* 2012. Retrieved November 25, 2012. http://s3.amazonaws.com/mcdbestof-section-pdfs/1/MCD_076_BOG _FINAL-ART_04.pdf

McDonough, W., and M. Braungart. *Cradle to Cradle.* New York, NY: North Point Press, 2002.

McDonough, W., and M. Braungart. *Upcycle.* North Point Press, 2023.

*McDonough, W., and Partners. *The Hannover Principles Design for Sustainability,* 1992. Retrieved March 28, 2013. www.mcdonough.com/principles.pdf.

McKinsey and Co. *Global Survey Results. The Business of Sustainability.* Sustainability and Resource Productivity Practice, 2011. www.mckinsey.com/ business-functions/sustainability-and-resource-productivity/our-insights/ the-business-of-sustainability-mckinsey-global-survey-results.

McKinsey and Co. *Consumers Care About Sustainability—and Back it Up With Their Wallets,* 2023. Retrieved May 29, 2024. www.mckinsey.com/~/ media/mckinsey/industries/consumer%20packaged%20goods/our%20 insights/consumers%20care%20about%20sustainability%20and%20 back%20it%20up%20with%20their%20wallets/consumers-care-about-sustainability-and-back-it-up-with-their-wallets-final.pdf?shouldIndex=false.

Meadows, D. H. *Thinking in Systems: A Primer.* White River Junction, VT: Chelsea Green Publishing, 2008.

Melnyk, S. A. *Measurements, Metrics and the Value-Driven Operations Management System.* Atlanta, GA: Lionheart Publications, 1999.

Melnyk, S. A., E. W. Davis, R. E. Spekman, and J. Sandor. "Outcome Driven Supply Chains." *Sloan Management Review* 51, no. 2 (2010): 33–38.

Melnyk, S. A., C. Peters, T. Schoenherr, and J. Miller. "Earned Preferential Treatment: The Reward for being a "Good" Customer." *Supply Chain Management Review.* March/April 2021, 40–47.

*Missimer M. *Social Sustainability Within the Framework for Strategic Sustainable Development.* Doctoral dissertation series No. 2015:09, Blekinge Institute of Technology, Department of Strategic Sustainable Development, Karlskrona, Sweden, 2015.

MIT Sloan Management Review & Boston Consulting Group. *The Innovation Bottom Line: Findings from the 2012 Sustainability and Innovation Global Executive Study and Research Report,* 2013

MIT Sloan Management Review and Boston Consulting Group. *Sustainability Nears a Tipping Point: Findings from the 2011 Sustainability and Innovation Global Executive Study and Research Report,* 2012. Retrieved March 22, 2013. http://c4168694.r94.cf2.rackcdn.com/MIT-SMR-BCG-Sustainability-Nears-a-Tipping-Point-Winter-2012.pdf.

*Mohin, T. "How Sustainability is Driving Employee Engagement and the Bottom Line." *Greenbiz.com,* September 29, 2011.

*Moore, G. *Crossing the Chasm.* New York, NY: Harper Business.1991.

Mubarik, M., and M. Shahbaz. *Blockchain Driven Supply Chain Management,* Springer. 2023.

*Nattrass, B., and M. Altomare. *The Natural Step for business: Wealth, Ecology and the Evolutionary Corporation.* Gabriola Island, BC: New Society Publishers, 1999.

Natural Capitalism Solutions. *Sustainability pays: Studies that prove the business case for sustainability,* 2012. Retrieved March 22, 2013. http://www.natcapsolutions.org/.

OECD. *OECD Due Diligence Guidance for Responsible Supply Chains of Minerals from Conflict-Affected and High-Risk areas.* Oecd.org. 2013. Retrieved February 8, 2013. "OECD Due Diligence Guidance for Responsible Supply Chains of Minerals from Conflict-Affected and High-Risk Areas".

*PE International. *PE International Handbook for Life Cycle Assessment Using the Gabi Education Software Package,* PE International. 2010. Retrieved March 28, 2013. www.gabi-software.com/fileadmin/gabi/tutorials/Paper-clip_Tutorial_Handbook_4.4.pdf.

Phipps, J. "Ten Worst Companies in terms of Social and Environmental Responsibility," *Baby Earth,* 2019. January 13, 2019. www.babyearth.com/blogs/grow/ten-worst-companies-social-environmental-responsibility.

*Polonsky, M., P. Rosenberger, and A. Ottman. "Stakeholder's Contribution to the Green New Product Development Process." *Journal of Marketing Management* 14 (1998): 533–557.

Porter, M. E., and M. R. Kramer. "Creating Shared Value." *Harvard Business Review* 89, no. ½ (2011): 62–77.

ProcurementIntelligenceUnit. *Byprocurementintelligencestaff.* 2011. Retrieved March 22, 2013. www.procurementleaders.com/news-archive/news-archive/failure-to-mitigate-supply-chain-risk-to-cost-companies-billions-in-2012.

Puma. "Puma completes first environmental profit and loss account which values impacts at € 145M," 2011. Retrieved March 22, 2013. http://about.puma.com/puma-completes-first-environmental-profit-and-loss-account-which-values-impacts-at-e-145-million/.

PWC. "The SEC's Climate Disclosure Rules are the Latest to Require Expanded ESG Reporting," 2024. Retrieved May 29 2024. www.pwc.com/us/en/services/esg/library/sec-climate-disclosures.html?WT.mc_id=CT3-PL300-DM1-TR1-LS2-SC_XS-CL-CN_SUSTAIN-Google&gclid=Cj0KCQjwmMayBhDuARIsAM9HM8d_kZUN0ai8KwoJmMmjj3jksax3L5M58bvngtC2hxNC6UM3h_9rKzQaAoOkEALw_wcB&gclsrc=aw.ds.

*Raelin, J. "Does Action Learning Promote Collaborative Leadership?" *Academy of Management Learning and Education* 5, no. 2 (2006): 152–168.

*Ravi, V., and R. Shankar "Analysis of Interactions Among the Barriers of Reverse Logistics." *Tech Forecast & Social Change* 72, no. 8 (2005): 1011–1029.

*Read, R. Dr. Russel Read, written testimony prepared for the U.S. senate banking subcommittee on securities, insurance and investment. In *The Way Out: Kick-Starting Capitalism to Save our Economic Ass,* edited by H. Lovins and B. Cohen (New York, NY: Hill and Wang Publishing, 2007), 42. New York, NY: Hill and Wang Publishing, 2007.

Saaty, T. L. "How to Make a Decision—The Analytic Hierarchy Process." *European Journal of Operational Research* 48,(1990): 9–26.

Science Based Targets initiative (SBTi). Retrieved May 29, 2024. https://sciencebasedtargets.org/.

*Scientific Applications International Corporation (SAIC). *Life Cycle Assessment: Principles and Practice.* 2006. Retrieved May 13, 2011. www.epa.gov/nrmrl/lcaccess/pdfs/600r06060.pdf.

*Schein, E. *Organizational Culture and Leadership.* Fort Worth, TX: Harcourt College Publishers, 1993.

Schwarz, A. "Best Brands for Social Impact." *Forbes,* April 16, 2024. www.forbes.com/lists/best-brands-social-impact/?sh=297c08231f90

Scott, M. "100 Most Sustainable Companies of 2023 Still Flourishing in Tumultuous Times." *Corporate Knights.* 2023. January 18, 2023. www.corporateknights.com/rankings/global-100-rankings/2023-global-100-rankings/2023-global-100-most-sustainable-companies/.

*Senge, P., B. Lichtenstein, K. Kaeufer, H. Bradbufy, and J. Carroll. "Collaborating for Systemic Change." *Sloan Management Review* 48, no. 2 (2007): 44–53.

Sheffi, Y. The New (Ab) Normal: Reshaping Business Supply Chains Strategy Beyond COVID-19, *MIT CLM Media,* 2020.

Shrivastava, P. "Green Supply Chain Management: A State-of-the-art Literature Review." *International Journal of Management Reviews* 9, no. 1 (2007): 53–80. https://19january2017snapshot.epa.gov/climatechange/social-cost-carbon.html.

Sourcemap.com. *The platform for open supply chains*, 2024. Retrieved May 29, 2024. https://open.sourcemap.com/.

*Spekman, R. E., and R. P. Hill. "Strategy for Effective Procurement in the 1980s." *Journal of Purchasing and Materials Management*, Winter (1980): 2–7.

*Sroufe, R. P. Effects of Environmental Management Systems on environmental management practices and operations. *Production and Operations Management*, 12, no. 3 (2003): 416–432.

*Sroufe, R. P. "Operationalizing Sustainability." *Journal of Sustainable Studies*, 1.1 (2016).

*Sroufe, R., R. Atkins, and S. Curkovic. "Purchasing and Supply Management Empowerment in the New Product Development Process." *International Journal of Value Chain Management* 14, no. 4 (2023): 459–480.

Sroufe, R. P., S. Curkovic, F. L. Montabon, and S. A. Melnyk. "The New Product Design Process and Design for the Environment: Crossing the chasm." *International Journal of Operations and Production Management* 20, no. 2 (2000): 267–291.

Sroufe, R. P. *Integrated Management: How Sustainability Creates Value for Any Business*, Emerald, 2018. https://books.emeraldinsight.com/page/detail/Integrated-Management/?k=9781787145627.

S&P. ESG Data Intelligence. 2024a. Retrieved May 29, 2024. www.spglobal.com/esg/solutions/esg-data-intelligence.

S&P. Global ESG Scores, 2024b. Retrieved May 29. www.spglobal.com/marketintelligence/en/solutions/sustainability-capital-iq-pro-platform#:~:text=Environmental%2C%20Social%20and%20Governance%20Raw%20Data%20Access,we%20assess%20in%20the%20S&P%20Global%20CSA.

*Stanislawski, R., and A. Szymonik. *Supply Chains in Reverse Logistics – The Process Approach for Sustainability and Environmental Protection*, Routledge. 2024.

Starbucks. *Responsibly Grown Coffee*, 2013. Retrieved March 22, 2013. www.starbucks.com/responsibility/sourcing/coffee.

Starbucks. Global Impact Report, 2023. Retrieved 2023 May 29, 2024. https://stories.starbucks.com/uploads/2024/02/2023-Starbucks-Global-Impact-Report.pdf.

*Stika, N. *Sustainability Drives Recruitment and Retention*, 2010. June 9 2010. www.cosemin-spring.com; Mindspring.com, topics, sustainability, greening.

*Supply Chain Operations Reference. *Supply Chain Operations Reference Model overview-version 10*, 201. Retrieved January 17, 2013. www.sup-ply-chain.org/

*Sustainable Land Development Initiative (SLDI) Code™, 2013. Retrieved April 2, 2013. www.sldi.org/.

Sustainable Accounting Standards Board (SASB). Materiality Maps, 2024. Retrieved May 29 2024. https://sasb.ifrs.org/standards/materiality-map/.

*The Natural Step: www.thenaturalstep.org/.

*The Natural Step International. *Sustainability Life Cycle Assessment Project Report.* Project Report. Stockholm: The Natural Step International, 2010.

*The Story of Stuff, Annie L. Retrieved May 29, 2024. www.storyofstuff.org/movies/story-of-stuff/.

*Touw, P. Chairman and CEO, ICIX, presentation 9/27/2012, *The New Metrics of Sustainable Business.* Sustainable Brands Conference, Presentation re- Marks. 2012. "The Future of Technology Networks in Sustainability".

*United Nations Global Compact and Business for Social Responsibility. *Supply chain sustainability: A practical guide for continuous improvement*, 2010. Retrieved July 12, 2013. http://supply-chain.unglobalcompact.org/site/article/68

United Nation's Sustainable Development Goals. https://sustainabledevelopment.un.org/sdgs

U.S. Securities and Exchange Commission. *Implementing Dodd-Frank Wall Street reform and consumer protection act—Pending Action*, 2013. Retrieved March 22, 2013. www.sec.gov/spotlight/dodd-frank/dfactivity-upcoming.shtml#11-12-11.

Underwriters Laboratory and GreenBiz Group. *UL 880: Standard for Sustainability, Manufacturing Organizations* (1st ed.) 2011. Retrieved July 11, 2012. www.ul.com/global/eng/pages/offerings/businesses/environment/services/sq/enterprisestandards/UL880/.

*UPS. "Sustainability at UPS Report." Retrieved July 25, 2012. https://about.ups.com/us/en/newsroom/press-releases/sustainable-services/ups-to-mark-world-environment-day-by-matching-offsets-of-carbon-neutral-shipments-in-june.html#:~:text=The%20per%20package%20flat%20rate,3%20Day%20Select%C2%AE%20services.

Walsh, J. "U.S. Natural Disasters Cost $145 Billion In 2021—3rd-Costliest Year On Record." *Forbes.* Accessed May 29, 2024. www.forbes.com/sites/joewalsh/2022/01/10/us-natural-disasters-cost-145-billion-in-2021---3rd-costliest-year-on-record/?sh=c1869f746065.

*Whelan, T., and E. Douglas. "How to Talk to Your CFO About Sustainability." *Harvard Business Review* 99, no, 1 (2021): 86–93.

*Willard, B. *The New Sustainability Advantage, 10th Anniversary Edition.* Canada: New Society Publishers, 2012.

Womack, J. P., D. T. Jones, and D. Roos. *The Machine that Changed the World.* New York, NY: Free Press, 1990.

World Business Council for Sustainable Development 2024. www.wbcsd.org.

World Business Council for Sustainable Development. *Guide to corporate ecosystem valuation.* 2011. Retrieved May 29, 2024. www.wbcsd.org/Archive/ Assess-and-Manage-Performance/Resources/Guide-to-Corporate-Ecosystem -Valuation.

*Zimon, D., J. Tyan, and R. Sroufe. "Drivers of Sustainable Supply Chain Management: Practices to Alignment With UN SDGs." *International Journal for Quality Research* 14, no. 1 (2020).

Index

About the Authors

Robert P. Sroufe is the Falk Chair of Socially Responsible Business at Chatham University. Within the top-ranked Falk School of Sustainability and Environment, he is responsible for delivering courses on sustainable business practices for innovation and management applications while developing graduate academic consulting projects every semester with corporate sponsors. He is a researcher and consultant in operationalizing integrated management and sustainable business practices, strategic sustainability, environmental management systems, decarbonization, high-performance buildings, and aligning the UN SDGs with business performance.

Steven A. Melnyk is a professor of operations and supply chain management at Michigan State University. He has coauthored 20 books on operations and supply chain management and over 90 journal articles. He sits on the editorial review boards for *Production and Inventory Management, Journal of Supply Chain Management, Journal of Humanitarian Logistics and Supply Chain Management* (where he is coauthor for North America), and *International Journal of Production Research*. His research focus includes supply chain risk and resilience, strategic supply chain management, behavioral research, and certified management standards.

www.ingramcontent.com/pod-product-compliance
Lightning Source LLC
Chambersburg PA
CBHW061200220326
41599CB00025B/4549